Dealing
With
Weeds

What if your life could be more fruitful
through less not more?

LUNGILE NCUBE

WESTBOW
PRESS®
A DIVISION OF THOMAS NELSON
& ZONDERVAN

WestBow Press books may be ordered through booksellers or by contacting:

WestBow Press
A Division of Thomas Nelson & Zondervan
1663 Liberty Drive
Bloomington, IN 47403
www.westbowpress.com
844-714-3454

ISBN: 978-1-6642-5752-8 (sc)
ISBN: 978-1-6642-5751-1 (hc)
ISBN: 978-1-6642-5753-5 (e)

Library of Congress Control Number: 2022902378

Print information available on the last page.

WestBow Press rev. date: 03/08/2022

Contents

Contents

Introduction

I still remember the day when my wife came to me, unexpectedly, and said, "I'd like to start a garden." Now this statement on its own should not be frightening to hear. However, considering the season that my wife, Zinty and I were in, it didn't make much sense. We were in the middle of one of the busiest and most demanding seasons of our lives. We had recently moved to a new city, began running a community centre and, to cap it all off, we were now only a few months away from planting a church. It was obvious to me that we did not have much in the way of margin to start a garden (or so I thought). We both loved what we were doing, and we were excited about the new season of church planting. We were not sad or stressed about it. However, we both knew fully well that this was going to be a season of being 'all hands to the pump' for both of us.

This is the reason why when Zinty came to me on that day and said, "I would like to start an herb garden," I had a moment that I'm sure many of us can relate with. A thousand different possible responses to that question went through my mind in almost an instant, none of which would have been sensitive to say at that very moment. So, I found myself responding by simply saying, "OK." On the inside, I felt far from OK. I was asking myself how she was planning to squeeze in extra time to buy seedlings, plant them, water them, weed around them and harvest them. Then there was the million-dollar question- what would she then use the herbs for? Please don't get me wrong. I liked the idea of my wife having a garden, but I did not see yet how that idea could be a reality. In the process of time, I eventually shared with her how I truly felt. I explained that I did not think she or we had the time for it based on the season of life that we were in.

Fast forward to today and I can tell you in hindsight that I was wrong. Emphatically wrong for that matter. As I sit down on my chair authoring this book, we (notice how the narrative has changed from me to we :-)) have had a beautiful herb garden. It has given us fresh herbs like parsley, fennel, coriander, origanum, marjoram, mint, kale, lavender, and my current favourite celery.

My wife eventually started the garden on her own, with me as a bit of a pessimistic spectator. However, over time, something in me changed. I found myself being drawn to the garden and spending more time with Zinty in it. Eventually, I started going into it by myself. I began to enjoy it and grew to love spending long periods of time there on my own. Using the garden, the Lord began to show me things that I had never seen before. I began to realise that some of my most sacred times with the Lord came when I was either alone or with my wife in the garden. Many messages that I eventually spoke to the church were birthed in the garden. The garden had such an impact on me that it became my go-to place. When I'd go there my head would become clear, my heart would be calmed, and my spirit would be refreshed. I had been quickly transformed from being the garden pessimist to becoming the chief gardener in our home.

It was during one of these times, while working in the garden, that the Lord began to show me things about weeds that I had never seen before. Initially it was about the weeds in the garden but eventually the Lord turned my attention to how it is the same with me as His child. I distinctly remember that day even as I author this book right now. I was in the garden weeding. I had been weeding the same area of the garden for a couple of days in a row but still hadn't managed to get rid of all the weeds. Because of this, I was beginning to get a little frustrated. I wasn't getting it done as fast as I had hoped. The work was more than I had estimated (isn't it always) and the progress felt slower than what I thought my work deserved.

In my moment of frustration, as all these thoughts went through my head, the Holy Spirit began to show me many insights concerning dealing with weeds in the garden of my life. As I continued working in the garden that day, my attitude changed from being in a hurry to being hungry to learn. Over the course of many days, weeks and even months I learnt from the Holy Spirit, through my experiences in the garden, the need for me to deal with weeds in my life. This book in many ways is a journal of the lessons He taught me in the garden.

The reason I am writing this book is because, on the 31st of December

2018, the Lord spoke to me during my devotional time. I was reading Revelation 1:11a (NLT) which says, ***"Write in a book everything you see and send it to the seven churches."*** As I did, these words became personal to me. The Lord impressed on my heart that I was to do the same with everything that I had seen in the garden. This is what I am doing. I hope these principles bring you the same joy and fruitfulness (and even more) that I have experienced as I've put them into practice. Over time, I've learned that the man was put in the garden, not for the benefit of the garden but for the benefit of the man. The garden makes the human being a better person. In the same way that Adam had to tend to a physical garden we are all dealing with spiritual gardens that God has entrusted to us. He did this because God desires to make us better people. He desires to make us more like Him and the gardens of our lives is one of the tools in His hand that He uses to make that happen. So just like I learned to embrace my (unwelcome) garden when my wife decided to start one, I hope you learn to embrace yours too. By His grace, may you become more fruitful through less, not more as the Lord completes the work that He started in you. Let's begin!

Enjoy!

Contained in this book are lessons that will help you:

1. Realise that we all have a garden
2. Learn the purpose of your garden
3. Define weeds correctly
4. Stop making excuses for not being fruitful
5. Learn the three categories of weeds
6. Learn how Jesus defines weeds
7. Learn the greater danger of weeds
8. Achieve 100 % fruitfulness
9. Change your mindset so you can deal with roots not just results of weeds
10. Retrace your steps so you can uproot weeds
11. Invite others to help you deal with weeds in your life
12. Learn the various kinds of weeds
13. Learn to use different strategies for various kinds of weeds
14. Measure fruitfulness correctly
15. Become a friend of sinners like Jesus was
16. Understand and show mercy to yourself and others
17. Learn from the Corinthian church to see people differently
18. To not be defeated by the enemy's strategies
19. Keep your heart soft
20. Develop repeatable routines for dealing with weeds
21. Maintain a love for your garden

SECTION I

WEEDS: WHY AND WHAT?

CHAPTER 1

❋

We All Have a Garden

"Indeed Israel is the vineyard of the LORD who commands armies, the people of Judah are the cultivated place in which he took delight."
Isaiah 5:7a (NET)

"I will plant them there with my own hands in order to bring myself glory." Isaiah 60:21b (NLT)

You Were Made to Be Fruitful

To understand and appreciate the need to deal with weeds, it is helpful to begin by understanding who you are. As a believer, you are the Lord's garden. When you were born again, a garden was planted in this world. A unique, beautiful garden. This garden was planted by "God's own hands," as explained in the two verses quoted above. And just as all gardens are unique, God crafted you to be a specific and special one-of-a-kind garden.

The reason God did this was for one specific purpose—*to bring Himself glory.* Yes, just as you and I like to show off our gardens to our visitors whenever we get an opportunity, God planted us as a garden to bring Himself glory. He likes to show us off as examples of how great He is (the Lord's conversation regarding Job is a great illustration of this, by

1

the way). Specifically, being used to "bring God glory" means that God desires to achieve three things through your life:

1. to show His beauty,
2. to reveal His greatness, and
3. to bring honor to His name.

Since we are a garden, we can conclude that we were made to be fruitful (all gardens are!). Doing these three things listed above is what fruitfulness looks like for us. In light of this, it is essential to view and treat our lives as gardens in the spiritual sense. This understanding that we are created as gardens is tied to fulfilling the very purpose for which we were created.

It is no wonder that five of the eighteen parables Jesus taught included a reference to plant life. That works out to almost a third of His teaching through parables. Undoubtedly, this is a sign pointing to the fact that as you learn to view and treat your life as a garden, you will position yourself to succeed in glorifying your Father in heaven. This is part of the reason Jesus taught His followers, saying, "When you bear a lot of fruit, it brings glory to my Father. It shows that you are my disciples" (John 15:8 NLT).

When reflecting on how God has created each of us as gardens, there are two observations that I found to be true of all of us; we each have responsibility and capability.

1. Responsibility: If we all have a garden, we all have a responsibility to deal with weeds! It is impossible to care for a garden and not need to deal with weeds.
2. Capability: A garden free of weeds and well taken care of will naturally produce good fruit and lots of it. It doesn't need to strive to do so. We don't hear plants screaming and squealing in the night, trying to grow and produce fruit (except bamboo, but it squeals for a different reason). We know that if they are healthy and undisturbed by weeds, gardens will produce a harvest at some point.

These two observations about all of us turned into a passion and a burden in my heart to help people know the truth about their capability and embrace the responsibility that comes with it. I believe that knowing and believing these truths about yourself will inspire you to love and care for your garden, which is your life. I am motivated to embark on this journey with you because, free of weeds, I am certain that your level of fruitfulness will increase. I am certain that your life can be more fruitful through less, not more, as you learn to remove weeds from your life. As the Lord's garden, you were created to be fruitful. You have it in you to be like a well-watered garden—a beautiful, pleasant garden that produces plenty of good fruit. In the rest of this chapter, we'll explore further the responsibility and capability that we each have as the Lord's very own garden!

Responsibility: Having a Garden Means Dealing with Weeds

Observe with me what Jesus says about levels of fruitfulness in His parable about sowing. "Other seeds fell on fertile soil, and they produced a crop that was thirty, sixty, and even a hundred times as much as had been planted!" (Matthew 13:8 NLT). Jesus highlighted that the fertile ground did not give the same yield. Instead, He said that when the seed fell on fertile ground, there were three levels of fruitfulness. This caught my attention. From my perspective, if the ground was fertile and the seed was the same, then the yield should have been the same. However, it was not. This means there is another variable that affects the levels of fruitfulness in addition to the quality of the seed and the fertility of the soil (which were both good in this instance.) I believe that variable is weeds (the way in which we deal with them, to be specific). To be fruitful we must realize the responsibility the Lord has given us to deal with weeds in the gardens of our lives. This is the third important contributing factor to our fruitfulness. People who deal with weeds effectively produce a crop that is a hundred times as much as what was planted by the seed of the Word of God in their hearts. Based on the differing levels of fruitfulness that Jesus prophesied through His parable, it seems that those who follow Jesus treat this responsibility differently.

For me, the realization that I have a garden to care for came through the experience that I narrated briefly in the introduction. Before my wife suggested the idea of a garden, we never had to deal with weeds. We never had to read up on how to effectively tackle a weed problem in a garden. We never had to bend our backs in the garden (sometimes in blazing hot savannah temperatures that can go past forty degrees Celsius). Our home life was free of all these kinds of cares and concerns. In other words, we did not have responsibility!

However, the moment we started a garden, our lives changed. If we were going to harvest something (more like anything, sometimes) we needed to make time to deal with weeds in our garden. This responsibility changed our lives in many ways. It changed how we

- spent our time,
- spent our money (those seedlings do not rain from the sky, if you know what I mean),
- thought and felt about the weather (there's nothing like a shower from heaven just when you were about to go and water the garden), and
- planned our meals (when the celery is ready, then it's the celery that's going to be served!).

As you can see, a lot changed in our lives when we took on the responsibility of having a garden. It was a complete shift in perspective and lifestyle. Even the most basic parts of our lives were affected. If we wanted our garden to be fruitful, it was impossible for us to continue living our lives the way we had always done before we planted it. As I reflected on all these changes to our lives, it dawned on me that my life is a garden! Verses that I had read in the Bible before and skimmed over became more alive to me in my garden moments. I began to realize that this life that I have is a garden planted by the Lord's very own hands. Almost immediately I also began to realize how, oftentimes, I lived as if I did not own a garden. I lived like Zinty, and I did before we had our garden, and yet I already had a garden. When I saw my life from this perspective, it quickly became obvious to me how damaging this was. I realized that in life the question is never *if* I am dealing with weeds. Rather, the question always is *how*

4

I am dealing with my weeds. By virtue of being alive, you and I have responsibility. That responsibility is a garden entrusted to us by our Father in heaven. Having this garden means you and I are not and cannot be exempt from dealing with weeds.

This gave me an urgency to change my approach to my life and the weeds that come with it. I would like to challenge you to make the same changes as we begin. When it comes to the ongoing responsibility of dealing with weeds in our lives, I've noted three kinds of approaches. My challenge is that we would take the approach that produces the most fruit. Let's look closer at the three kinds of approaches.

1. Abdicating our responsibility: Most people deal with weeds passively. They live life almost as if weeds don't exist. It doesn't take long to learn that denying something's existence doesn't stop that thing from affecting your life! A denial of weeds doesn't stop them from destroying the garden of my life. In fact, there's no fruit for those who abdicate their responsibility of dealing with weeds.

2. Tolerating our responsibility: Few people deal with weeds occasionally. They do not deny their responsibility to deal with weeds. However, for one reason or another, they do not treat this responsibility with the seriousness that it deserves. We all know that if a garden is to be fruitful, we must consistently care for it by removing weeds. This can't be something we do only once in a while when the time is right or we're in the mood. The result, if our approach is to take on our responsibility to deal with weeds occasionally, is that we will only be partially fruitful.

3. Embracing our responsibility: Even fewer people consistently and proactively deal with weeds. You are (or can be) this kind of person—the one who aspires to be in the "even fewer" category. I believe this because you picked up this book, and I commend you for it. I believe this because you set aside time to read it and you followed through on it as you are doing right now, and I commend you for it. My hope is that you find truths in this book that will equip you as you pursue all that God has given you through Jesus Christ. My hope for you is fruitfulness.

Dealing with weeds effectively helps us stop wasting nutrition that is meant for the seed on weeds. This is essential because no matter how much nutrition I give to a weed it will never become a seed. Instead, it just grows bigger allowing it to hurt and hinder me more forcefully. This is why our lives often become more fruitful through less not more. A key principle for living a fruitful life is learning the secret of giving nutrition (our energy, time, emotional investment, and everything else) to the right things, not everything. If we faithfully give nutrition to everything that calls for our attention the result will be burnout, instead of an increase in fruitfulness. Our lives are gardens, and, in a garden, a wise farmer learns to remove weeds so that his plants can flourish and be more fruitful. So, in the garden of life, may you be the farmer who is wise enough to remove weeds so that your life becomes more fruitful. May you be the kind of farmer who neither abdicates nor tolerates his responsibility; giving nutrition to the right things by learning to embrace your responsibility to deal with weeds!

2. Capability

More Than Just Spectators in The Arena of Destiny

Because we were created in the image of God, we all have the capability to be fruitful, and yet there are many who fail to realise this. Failure to realise, accept and live according to this truth is one of life's biggest tragedies. It makes the enemy's job of stifling our fruitfulness a lot easier. It is like me and Zinty trying to keep our former life pattern even after planting our garden. For example, by eating meals that are lacking in vegetables when we have vegetables growing in our garden. If you saw us do this, you would consider us unwise. Yet there are many of us who come to a relationship with Jesus and still try to live lives that do not embrace the essential truth that we possess the capability to be fruitful.

The root that often causes us to fail to embrace our capability is found in how we view ourselves. We think that others are capable of fruitfulness but, for some reason, we are not. We might think this is because of our genes, past mistakes, or education level. We view ourselves as not being talented enough or talented at all. We minimise or completely disregard our unique capabilities as individuals. The result of this negative self-view is that we don't embrace the capability that we have to make a difference in this world. This mentality causes us to view ourselves as spectators in the arena of destiny. Spectators who only get to watch other 'superstar believers' walk in the power of God. We treat them like celebrities as we admire them by liking their posts on social media and participating in their gatherings without also playing our part. (Cheering one another on and supporting other believers is a right and important practice. This is not what I am talking about here.) What I am talking about is sitting on the couch, believing that I have nothing to offer and looking on while others live out their lives before me. This is wrong and yet many followers of Jesus Christ are following Him with this mentality; a mentality that denies the capability that the Lord has put in each one of us. The result is that we don't concern ourselves with the important work of weeding. We are guilty by virtue of neglect. This kind of living does not glorify God.

Uniquely Created to Bring God Glory

The truth is that God has given us all capability. This is the reason He deserves glory from our lives. We are uniquely created by God to bring Him glory. He has placed treasures in us that, when expressed, reveal just how good He is as a Creator and Father. This is a reality seen throughout His Word especially in Paul's letter to the Corinthians when he declared that *"Each person is given something to do that shows who God is; Everyone gets in on it, everyone benefits. All kinds of things are handed out by the Spirit, and to all kinds of people." (1 Corinthians 12:7 MSG)*

My favourite part of this declaration is the part where Paul emphasizes that "Everyone gets in on it" Paul had already said in the previous sentence that "each person is given something," and yet he chooses to emphasize it further by declaring that "Everyone gets in on it." Whenever we see the Word of God repeat something it is for our benefit. It is because what is being mentioned matters so much it is worth saying twice. It matters for you and me to hear, understand and believe that every single one of us has capability. You have something that God planted in your life; something so beautiful and so unique at the same time. And when that thing is expressed, people look and say, "This is good," "God is good!" You have something that when you do, no one else on Earth can do it quite like you do. It's as unique as your fingerprint; there is none like it in all the world and no-one can reproduce it even if they spent all their life trying. It is as beautiful and unique as the beauty of your appearance. Yes, it's you I'm talking to; not just your friend or neighbour; you. You are BEAUTIFUL!

Embracing this truth is the beginning of seeing your life as a garden that God planted to bring Himself glory. This is expressed beautifully when Paul writes, *"For we are His workmanship, created in Christ Jesus for good works, which God prepared beforehand that we should walk in them." Ephesians 2:10 NKJV* You and I are God's workmanship; God's work of art; God's masterpiece! There is not a single one of us who came into this world empty. That is the beauty and power of our Creator; He hasn't yet (and never will) run out of creativity. This is what the book of Romans is teaching us when Paul says, *"In His grace, God has given us different gifts for doing certain things well. "Romans 12:6a NLT.* God has created the people in His kingdom differently. There are no two people who are the same. We have all been given:

1. Gifts
2. Talents
3. A calling(purpose).

In short, every human being was made to fulfil a specific purpose and we all received specific gifts and talents to help us fulfil that purpose. This is our garden. If we use our gifts and talents well, we will fulfil our calling (tend to our garden) and we will have fruit. This fruit is people; people that have had their lives made better (ministered to) because you fulfilled your calling (the life God intended for you- your garden). Through this, God is being glorified, since He is the one who planted the garden in the first place. This is how people see His greatness and beauty. This is how you inspire people to praise him- all from the garden of your life. This is what Jesus meant when He declared, *"The fruit that they (you) harvest is people brought to eternal life." John 4:36b NLT{Emphasis added by author};* When you live the life God created you to live you shine a light so powerful that it helps bring people to eternal life! That is fruitfulness.

The rest of this book becomes more valuable when you understand and embrace these two realisations about yourself. You have the capability to be fruitful and you have responsibility because you own a garden. This will save you from the enemy's strategies. The enemy knows that when we fail to realise that we have a garden in the spiritual sense it is inevitable that we will live our lives with a lack of intentionality that causes us to be unfruitful. This unfruitfulness is often incorrectly attributed to outside circumstances like the economy, our upbringing, our education or even our genetic makeup. However, the reality is that it is being fuelled by how we view our lives. So guard your mindset. Do not fall into the trap of viewing your life like a person who doesn't embrace the responsibility of weeding his garden and yet hopes to have a fruitful harvest when it is time for reaping. Just as there is no wisdom in this kind of thinking in the natural sense of farming it is unwise for you to approach your life this way. Following Jesus is fruitful when we do it with the mindset of a farmer. And every farmer needs to concern himself with weeds if he is to be fruitful. My hope and invitation to you is that you would be that kind of farmer. Keep in mind that when your life view changes for the better, your fruitfulness will be positively affected. There truly is tremendous power in how you view yourself.

Conclusion

As we will see further on, there is work involved in dealing with weeds and sometimes that work is challenging. But when we see ourselves as gardeners, these challenges go from being unexpected to obvious. They go from unnecessary to essential. They go from annoying to energising. All because we see ourselves differently. We see ourselves with the mentality that says, "I am an owner, I have been given a garden to tend to, that garden is my life, and my work is revealed precisely for what it is in the garden of my life."

Taken positively, this ownership mentality helps change how we view even the most mundane of tasks. It helps you to view them not as a hired hand but as an owner and that change affects everything. With the right mindset you can benefit from even the most humble and mundane tasks in life. With the right mindset, even the most mundane tasks can be extremely rewarding overall. This sets you up well to be fruitful because, after all, life is filled with many mundane and repetitive tasks. So instead of dreading them and wishing they would somehow disappear, it is better for us to learn to do them with a different mentality. One that helps us benefit from these mundane and repetitive tasks overall. The understanding of being an owner (RESPONSIBILITY) and the mentality that it creates (CAPABILITY- I CAN BE FRUITFUL) help us make this crucial shift towards fruitfulness. And this is what separates the fruitful believers from the unfruitful ones.

REFLECTION

As we conclude this chapter, here are four reflection questions for you to answer that will help you put into practice what you just read.

- How am I managing my responsibility to deal with weeds? Am I abdicating, tolerating, or embracing my responsibility?

  _____

  _____

  _____

  _____

  _____

- What is one change that I can make to bring myself to a place of embracing my responsibility with weeds?

  _____

  _____

  _____

  _____

  _____

- "Because we were created by God, we all have the capability as His gardens to be fruitful, and yet there are many who fail to realise this." How well do you think you understand your capability to be fruitful?

_____

_____

_____

_____

CHAPTER 2

❈

How to Define Weeds

"As the workers slept, his enemy came
and planted weeds among the wheat, then
slipped away." Matthew 13:25b NLT

Clarity Gives Energy
(Zinty Ncube)

Diagnosis Before Treatment

I believe in definitions. One of my personal beliefs in life is "to successfully solve it, I must first define it." I've learnt this from observing many areas of life. For example, before doctors treat us, they first diagnose us. There is no treatment that is so powerful that it eliminates the need for diagnosis. In diagnosing the patient, a doctor is defining what the problem is before proceeding to deal with it through medication. The same applies when dealing with weeds- to successfully deal with them, we must first diagnose them. Proper diagnosis is not only important, but also energising. This is because it gives us clarity and, like my wife Zinty once expressed to me, "clarity gives energy." In all the areas of our lives where we gain clarity, we find that we become energised, and that energy motivates us to improve. We need to gain clarity on many things including gaining clarity on what the real problem is in a given situation. In this section I would like to help us find clarity in our journey of fruitfulness by helping us define weeds. As we define them, we can identify and deal with them in our own lives. Let me begin by sharing the story of how I learnt the importance of defining weeds- defining them with clarity.

When I first made the commitment to author this book, I was excited (some might even say over-excited). I would always bring it up in conversation with Zinty. Somehow, I always found an excuse to bring it up in conversations even when the topic had nothing to do with weeds. I spent a lot of time journaling and preparing the material that I was going to write in the book. Authoring this book seemed like something that was going to be a breeze. I was so motivated that everything I did as I prepared to author the book felt like it was happening without much effort. I honestly thought that I would have the book written in a couple of days. However, as time went on, I began to spend less time on the book. Other things began to grab my attention. It didn't happen instantly. It was more of a gradual process. I began to spend less time writing as I focused on other things that I needed to do. I spoke about it less to Zinty. I brought it up less often in conversation. What is interesting is that I did not replace authoring this book with sinful things. No! It was simply good, normal everyday things that were not bad in themselves but resulted in me having less time to author a book- the book that I sincerely felt the Lord had called me to write. This went on for days. The days became weeks. The weeks turned into months. The months turned into years- almost two years to be exact!

Then one day, unexpectedly, Zinty brought up the book in conversation (notice that it was not me who brought it up this time :-)). As she asked me about my progress, I noticed myself becoming defensive. I don't really remember what excuse I gave for not having made progress on it. I do remember that it involved saying things like, "I would like to write it, but I have a lot of things on my plate right now." Zinty, in her response to my excuse, went straight to the heart of why I wasn't making any progress in authoring the book. She simply said that she felt there were things in my life that didn't need to be there. And that if I removed them I would have more than enough time to make progress and finish the book. As she was talking, a light bulb came on and I began to realise exactly what was going on. I was not making progress on authoring a book about dealing with weeds because I needed to deal with weeds in my own life. Weeds in my life were showing up at a deeper level. They stood in the way of me glorifying God in a new and deeper way by putting to paper the truths that He was speaking to me concerning weeds. Zinty was calling me out on the hypocrisy of my ways, and she didn't even know it.

I wasn't overly excited to hear what she was saying because as true as it was, it was also uncomfortable. My inaccurate definition of weeds was causing me to live a life where I could teach about weeds without having fully dealt with them in my own life. I did not lack zeal or enthusiasm for authoring this book and yet I wasn't making as much progress on it as I could. Thankfully, by the mercy and grace of God, I continued to deal with weeds in my life. The result was that there was enough room (and more to spare) for me to begin devoting myself to authoring this book and today you have it in your hand (or on your device). This experience wasn't just uncomfortable for discomfort's sake, it taught me an important lesson. HOW I DEFINE WEEDS MATTERS! Oftentimes this may be the difference between dealing with them effectively, so they are completely removed from our gardens or continuing to give excuses for having them in our lives leading to a life that is unfruitful (that is not bringing God glory.

Poor Definitions Lead to Excuses

In the same way that a poor diagnosis by a doctor will cause people to continue to suffer in their sickness while taking medicine that they hope will make them better, poor definitions of weeds cause us to suffer the effects of weeds while thinking we are free of them. We find ourselves living a life where we constantly give excuses- excuses for why we continue to live a mediocre life, excuses for why we keep putting off our dreams for another day, excuses for why we are producing so much less fruit in our garden than what we were created to produce.

I will also add that the knowledge of how to deal with weeds is most useful if I can identify weeds in my own life. Otherwise, this information is used to point a finger at others without practicing it in my own life. It is much easier to identify weeds in my spouse's life, my children, my pastor, or my boss at work. However, it is much more helpful (though humbling) to identify the weeds in my own life. This matters because it is extremely easy to be deceived into thinking, "I'm OK. I don't have to worry about weeds in my life; this is a message for someone else." I have never met somebody who couldn't get better at this. I have never met someone who has finished this journey of dealing with weeds once and for all. I realised that this is a journey that will last all our lives in the same way that a farmer never ceases to deal with weeds. Said another way, the only garden that no longer needs to concern itself with weeds is the one that no longer concerns itself with fruitfulness.

So, as the Lord's Garden, let me challenge us to move from excuses to definitions. Where in your life could you possibly be at the excuse stage like I was when Zinty called me out? Could there maybe be a project that has been on pause for the past five years, and every time people ask you why you haven't finished it you respond with an excuse? What is the number of books that we started reading and never finished or the ones that we felt we needed to write but never got started? What is the state of our prayer lives and Bible reading? Do we find ourselves squeezing in our Bible reading and prayer time into a 'busy life' giving the excuse that we have become busier taking care of the kids, growing a church, or starting a business? Are there areas of your life where you used to be excited (maybe even over-excited) but for some reason all you do nowadays is give excuses for why you can't pursue that dream anymore? Are there areas where you're still excited and yet you don't seem to be making any progress?

On the other side of our excuses is a uniqueness that screams "God is good at what He does. God is a Master craftsman. Just look at how He made me!" Oftentimes we have looked at others and thought, "Wow, they must be superhuman." I observed that statement closely and realised that in saying that we are silently saying "I don't think that is possible for me." But the truth is God created each of us in such a way that there is a place where we flourish in such a manner that when people look at us, they can't help but exclaim, "Oh man, she/he must be superhuman." This is the hope that I have as I author this book. I hope that as we learn God's definition of weeds we will go from EXCUSES TO DEFINITIONS, from wishes to winning and from ideas to execution. That is where our gardens begin to bear the fruit that God planted them for (His glory)!

Conclusion: Adding Knowledge to our Zeal

As you can see from these experiences, if we do not define weeds correctly, dealing with them is likely going to be futile. The result of misdiagnosing our weed problem (or any problem for that matter) is that, despite investing much effort into fixing it, we get little or no positive result. This leads to discouragement and, if this cycle is repeated many times, can even result in depression. In short, it is not a lack of effort but oftentimes misdirected effort that results in some of the discouragement we experience on our faith journey. As Proverbs 19:2 teaches us, *"Even zeal is no good without knowledge, and he who hurries his footsteps misses the mark." (Berean Study Bible).* As noble as our eagerness is, in dealing with weeds we ought to add knowledge to it, so we don't miss the mark that God planted us to hit- FRUITFULNESS!

So, if my life has areas of constant discouragement and depression this may NOT be the result of lacking zeal and desire to change and get better. It may be the fruit of misdiagnosed weeds. This may be the result of neglected areas in our hearts that are being choked by weeds. That is why I passionately believe in us understanding and clearly defining what weeds are in the garden of our hearts. We NEED to learn to see them in our lives if we are to correctly deal with them. And when it comes to correctly dealing with weeds (and many other areas of our lives) *zeal is no good without knowledge.* So, in our effort to add knowledge to our zeal, let's look at the dictionary definition of a weed.

CHAPTER 3

※

Definitions of Weeds

When our definitions match God's definitions we have begun to see clearly.

In the Webster 1913 dictionary a weed is defined this way:

Literal Definition: Any plant growing in cultivated ground to the injury of the crop or desired vegetation,

Figurative Definition: Something unprofitable or troublesome; anything useless.

As we can see from the definitions above, in nature, a weed will often injure and even destroy the more desirable plants from a garden. This mirrors their effect in the garden of our lives. If undealt with, weeds will grow vigorously and eventually choke out the more desirable fruit in us. This fruit represents traits that would have glorified God if they'd been nurtured to maturity. The result of this is that even though we profess faith in Jesus, our lives don't bring Him glory. The seed that He planted in our hearts has been choked out by other plants that grew more vigorously.

So, based on these definitions, if we are to properly define weeds, we must look at areas in our lives that are growing but not producing value. This means they tend to take up a lot of our time (overgrow) and stop us from developing other areas where we could be fruitful. All the while they do not produce any fruit. Weeds take away valuable time that we could be spending making progress on our dreams to one day author a book, record an album, or learn a new language. The list is endless.

Three Categories of Weeds

There are three categories of things that can be defined as weeds in the heart of a believer:

- the unholy
- the unhelpful
- the unpurposeful.

The unholy are the things that the Bible calls sin. These are things that the Word of God teaches and commands us not to do. The unhelpful are the things that, though not sinful, do not help us live a holy life. The Bible calls these weights. Other translations call them hindrances. We see a brief description of these two categories of weeds in the book of Hebrews when the Bible says, *"...stripping off every unnecessary weight and the sin which so easily and cleverly entangles us, let us run with endurance and active persistence the race that is set before us," Hebrews 12:1 AMP.*

These two categories come with descriptions that give us more clues as we discover the nature and danger of weeds. When speaking of sin (the unholy), the Bible warns us that it "easily and cleverly entangles us." This is such a fitting description of weeds because when you work with gardens you realise quickly that weeds easily grow in a garden. In our lives this means that our battle with sin is a continuous one because of how easily and cleverly sin can entangle us. Those who think they are no longer in a battle to overcome sin are living in deception. As we are taught in the following verse, *"If we say, "We have no sin," we are deceiving ourselves, and the truth is not in us." 1 John 1:8 CSB* Every human being is in this battle of dealing with and overcoming weeds and the first area where that is done is in the area of all that can be categorised as sin. Thankfully, because of The One who overcame sin, there is hope that if we put our trust in Him, we will overcome sin.

Concerning the weights and hindrances (the unhelpful) the Bible defines them as unnecessary. This is like an example my pastor once gave of running a marathon while carrying a backpack filled with bricks. It may not be against the rules, but it will not help you be the first to the finish line. This category of weeds isn't against the rules, but it will stop us from being fruitful to the capacity that God created us. This may include some of our dietary choices, TV watching habits and sleep patterns. To deal with these kinds of weeds we need to first realise that it is possible to live our lives according to the rules and still be unfruitful. This is because our God is a God of productivity, not just activity. He desires to see us productive, and to be productive we often need to go beyond the rules to a standard where few people are willing to go. Because fewer people are willing to go there, there'll always be more room at the top levels of productivity than there is at the bottom levels of productivity. This is the heart behind Jesus' teaching on going the extra mile. Those willing to go the extra mile in pursuing holy living stand out because few people are willing to go the extra mile.

There is a third category of weeds which is the unpurposeful. In nature this can be illustrated by a tomato plant growing in a cabbage garden. As much as we love and enjoy tomatoes, in the context of a cabbage garden, the tomato is a weed. As gardens we each have specific purposes according to God's plan. In fact, by definition, a garden is not a garden unless what is growing in it is specific. Areas that have unspecific vegetation growing in them are called bushes. You are not the Lord's bush; you are the Lord's Garden. He has chosen very specific plants to grow in your garden. He says of you, ***"For I know the plans I have for you," declares the Lord, "plans to prosper you and not to harm you, plans to give you hope and a future." Jeremiah 29:11 NIV.*** Therefore, anything outside of that specific plan which I may be nurturing in the garden of my life, no matter how good, is a weed. The farmer of the cabbage garden has no choice but to uproot the tomato plant. In the same way, we are responsible to uproot the things growing in us that are not a part of God's specific plan for our lives no matter how good they are.

Lessons From a Soccer Match

I made this observation about weeds while watching an in-door soccer match. This was not a professional soccer match. It was being played for social and recreational purposes. The number of players available for this match was nine. Since nine is an odd number, it was impossible to split the teams evenly. As a result, one team had five players and the other had four. Once the players had been divided up into two teams, the match began. Interestingly, the team with four players proved stronger than the one with five players and was dominating the match. However, as the match was going on, another team started forming on the terraces and they needed one more team member to form a complete team. Since the team losing had one extra player, they decided to sacrifice one of their players for the team on the side-lines that had three players. To my surprise, this team, which had just lost a player, began playing better football. They managed to eventually turn the match around and beat their opponents who had been dominating the game for a while. They played much better football and scored more goals after losing one of their players. As I watched this, I realised that it is the same with weeds. Weeds are like that teammate who helps you play better when he is absent. Whether it is unholy, unhelpful or unpurposeful, there is one thing common to all weeds, our lives will be more fruitful without them.

This may seem surprising, but it happens more often that we realise. In the home, the dishes are cleaned faster when a few committed individuals decide 'enough is enough, we're going to clean this mess" (and oftentimes this may literally be one person out of the whole family). In the workplace, it takes a few dedicated team members to help the organisation achieve its goals for productivity and profitability. At church, it is the sacrificial giving of a few committed individuals that helps the church break even financially. And so it is with our lives; oftentimes we will achieve more with less. The secret lies in distinguishing between:

- the holy and the unholy
- the helpful and the unhelpful
- what is my purpose and what is not?
- what is major and what is minor

- what is important and what is important now
- what is core and what is extra

As we do these things well, we will find that we are well set up for the journey of dealing with our weeds. This is the heart of this book- to help you live fruitfully by removing from the garden of life all those teammates who help you become fruitful by being absent from your garden. It is indeed true that in life, "less is more!" More often than not we are gaining when we lose something. The key is to lose the right things- the weeds. Our lives can truly be more fruitful through less not more.

CHAPTER 4

✳

Weeds as Defined by Jesus

Lessons from the Parables

In the Bible we see these three examples of weeds from Jesus' teachings:

- cares of this world
- deceitfulness of riches
- people

All three of these definitions are found in the 13ᵗʰ chapter of the Gospel of Matthew. Two are in the parable of the soils and one is in the parable of the wheat and the weeds (tares). The parable of the soils is a story that Jesus told to illustrate how different people respond when He plants His Word (represented by the seed) in the garden of our hearts (represented by the soil). We receive the Word of God through preaching, teaching, reading, and meditating on it. In the parable, the seed planted in each of the four soils was the same and yet some ground did not produce fruit at all and even the ground that was fruitful varied in the level of fruitfulness.

When speaking of one the soils Jesus said, *"Other seed fell among thorns, which grew up and choked the plants." Matthew 13:7 CJB.* In explaining what this represented he said, *"The seed falling among the thorns refers to someone who hears the word, but the worries of this life and the deceitfulness of wealth choke the word, making it unfruitful." (Matthew 13:22 NIV)* Jesus' explanation gives us things that can be defined as weeds in our lives.

1. The worries of this life
2. The deceitfulness of wealth.

It is no coincidence that Jesus chose to highlight these specific weeds during his time on earth. In His brief ministry on earth Jesus focused on what was major in every issue that He addressed. Weeds are no different. Therefore, Jesus' focus on these two may be a sign of the major battles that we have to overcome as we deal with weeds.

Worries of Life

Worries of life are legitimate needs and details of our lives that need to be taken care of. They are not unnecessary. They are good and necessary things for living our lives well. And when held in proper perspective they contribute positively to our livelihood and fruitfulness. However, beyond a certain point these legitimate needs and details can turn into worries. This results in them becoming distractions that take up a larger share of our time investment than God intended. And that is where the problem comes. You see, time is one of our most valuable resources for fulfilling our calling and when worries are present, some of that resource is wasted. And the problem with wasting time on the worries of life is that there is no way of getting that time back. Time is a non-renewable resource and therefore it is precious and must be used wisely if our lives are to be fruitful.

Legitimate needs and cares of life turn into worries of life when we do not manage them in a healthy and balanced way. This is what causes them to eventually become hindrances that can ultimately give birth to sin. An example of this is the ongoing need to make sure that I can provide for my family financially. Is it a legitimate need? Yes! Absolutely! But if we allow it to go from being a legitimate concern to a worry it becomes a weed that stops us being fruitful. It becomes the excuse for not stepping out in faith when God calls us to full time ministry or prompts us to give sacrificially. It gives birth to disobedient responses to the Lord as He leads us through His Holy Spirit. When we allow these legitimate concerns and others like it to turn into worries, we corner ourselves into feeling like we have no choice but to make God fit into the box of how we interpret life. We want Him to do things our way. We become safety-driven over being faith-driven (and we tell ourselves that we have a good excuse for it). Without intending to, we limit God, not because we are denying His existence but rather because we want Him to do things our way. This is the result of the weed of 'worries of this life.'

What legitimate concerns in your life have gone from being needs to becoming worries? Those may be the weeds that you need to deal with to become fruitful. And dealing with them will centre more around having a renewed perspective about them as opposed to removing them from your life completely. 'Worries of life' fits dead centre into the 'unhelpful kind of weeds' that we saw in the previous chapter.

Deceitfulness of Wealth

Jesus' second definition of weeds is the 'deceitfulness of wealth." In a different translation this weed is expressed this way, ***"the pleasure and delight and glamour and deceitfulness of riches" Matthew 13:20 AMPC.*** As you can see this is not about need anymore. This is about the extras of life that we don't need to have- we just want to have them. We just have to have them. By Jesus calling wealth deceitful he is saying that it tends to make us think we are ok when in fact we are not. We think we are being fruitful, but our gardens are in fact being choked to death. We think we have made it, but we actually have missed it. We have missed the mark for which God planted us. We are deceived!

I can relate to this from my time in our herb garden. It didn't take long for me to realise that weeds are a tricky customer. They need to be managed with the wisdom of a serpent like Jesus says. They are relentless, deceptive, and require hard work. By nature, they hide, and it takes a great deal of discipline and diligence to effectively remove them. When we are deceived by wealth, pleasure becomes more precious than prayer. We delight more in what we have acquired than in the God who helped us acquire it. We see this world as so glamorous that the world to come begins to feel a little less glamorous and a little less relevant in our lives. Because of this our best energies are invested in this world, not in the world to come. As a result, the seed of the Word of God is slowly choked until there is no fruit at all. And this can happen to the best of us if we poorly define weeds in our lives.

This was the case with the church in Laodicea. They thought they were ok because they possessed the riches of this world. But Jesus, when giving them an update on the current state of their lives, said, *"You say, 'I am rich. I have everything I want. I don't need a thing! 'And you don't realise that you are wretched and miserable and poor and blind and naked." Revelation 3:17 NLT.* These four descriptions of the Laodicean Church are reflective of what our lives can turn out to be if we allow ourselves to be deceived by riches; to be deceived by our ability to pay the biggest tithe in our church, our ability to give towards missions in another continent, or the ability to buy what we want to when we want to buy it and to have money to spare after that.

Obviously, it is not sin to be rich. However, when riches are not assessed correctly, they create lukewarm hearts that cause us to think, "If I'm prospering financially, it proves that God approves of my lifestyle, no matter how much I've actually strayed off the course He has marked out for me." Riches can deceive us into thinking we have arrived when God still wants us to press on to the mark of our high calling. We often refer to those who are rich by saying they have "made it." This statement, "they have made it," reveals the mentality we have towards being rich. We think, 'If somebody is rich, they are OK now.' And yet God is saying both to the poor and the rich, *"I advise you to buy gold from me-gold that has been purified by fire. Then you will be rich. Also buy white garments from me so you will not be shamed by your nakedness, and ointment for your eyes so you will be able to see." (Revelation 3:18 NLT)*

There is a gold that we can have which is better than the gold this world has to offer us. That is the gold God wants us to have. Pursuing and possessing the riches of this world can sometimes distract us from seeing our need for true gold. I am hoping that in learning about weeds, you and I will receive ointment for our eyes. This ointment will help us see clearly so we can purchase purified gold and white garments from Jesus. This way, we will not live in the constant shame that weeds can bring in our lives. This is a definition of weeds that is truly relevant for us who follow Jesus in the 21st century.

People- The Exception

Jesus' third definition of weeds is found in the parable of the wheat and the weeds. He told us, *"The Kingdom of Heaven is like a farmer who planted good seed in his field. 25 But that night as the workers slept, his enemy came and planted weeds among the wheat, then slipped away. 26 When the crop began to grow and produce grain, the weeds also grew." Matthew 13:24-26 NLT.* The Greek word translated weeds in this parable is zizanion. Zizanion is a type of weed that looks like wheat from a distance but produces poisonous black seeds. This teaches us that weeds can also be people who look like us but do not produce the fruit of the Spirit. In the same way that a weed in a natural garden did not come from the seed planted by the farmer, these people are not born of the seed of God's Word.

It is sobering to think that there are people planted in our churches, businesses, schools and lives by the enemy, the Devil. There are people that you and I rub shoulders with every day that the Devil, in his scheming, has positioned there. What is even more surprising is the farmer's response to this situation, *"An enemy has done this!' the farmer exclaimed. "Should we pull out the weeds?' they asked. "'No,' he replied, 'you'll uproot the wheat if you do. 30 Let both grow together until the harvest. Then I will tell the harvesters to sort out the weeds, tie them into bundles, and burn them, and to put the wheat in the barn.'" Mathew 13:28-30 NLT*

First of all, the farmer doesn't seem surprised by this. He seems to immediately know (without being told) that this was the work of an enemy. The farmer represents God and this teaches us that God isn't surprised by the enemy's scheming to plant weeds in our lives. After all, *"Nothing in all the world can be hidden from God. He can clearly see all things. Everything is open before him." Hebrews 4:13 ERV.* Knowing this should give us peace. Peace because we are assured that, while we do not always know the true nature of those around us, God knows fully well and is able to protect us where we need it. Indeed, *"The Lord knows those who belong to him," (2 Timothy 2:19b ERV)* and *"He takes care of those who trust him." (Nahum 1:7b ERV).*

Secondly, the farmer didn't allow his servants to uproot the weeds. The reason he gave was that he did not want to injure the wheat in any way.

The lesson here is that God will not uproot people planted in our lives by the Devil because that may cause us to be uprooted too! At first glance this may seem like it goes against the general understanding of weeds (that they choke and can even kill the plants). But in reality, there is a deeper lesson here. Jesus is teaching us that what the enemy intended to harm us (the enemy comes to steal, kill, and destroy us) God can turn around and use for our good if we respond correctly. God will use the roughness and unfairness of having to put up with people who are weeds to polish, refine and mould us into the likeness of Christ. It's also important to realise that when it comes to people, God's purpose is always that they should be saved. So, even when the enemy plants people as weeds in our lives, God's desire is that they should be saved. By leaving them in our lives, He gives us an opportunity to lead them to that salvation by the way we live. This is what Jesus meant when He declared, ***"You are the light of the world. A town built on a hill cannot be hidden … let your light shine before others, that they may see your good deeds and glorify your Father in heaven." Matthew 5:14& 16b NIV***

Let's look at Jesus as an example. A weed was planted among His twelve disciples. That weed was Judas. How did Jesus deal with this? Did he uproot Judas from the twelve and replace him with someone else who was going to be faithful and wouldn't betray him? No. Instead Jesus let the weed (Judas) grow with the seed (the rest of the disciples). When He gave them power to cast out demons, he gave it to Judas too. When He went around preaching the good news and healing the sick, He took Judas along too. When He washed His disciples' feet, He washed Judas' feet too. Even at the last supper, Judas was invited. He left by choice to betray Jesus. This may all look like it backfired on Jesus since Judas ended up betraying him. However, in betraying Jesus, Judas actually helped Him fulfil the purpose for which He had been sent by the Father to the earth- to offer Himself as a sacrifice for our sins. So, the lesson is simply this- the weeds that the enemy plants in our lives will be used by our Father to help us fulfil His purpose on earth. They will help us become even more fruitful. So, we must not fear those we think are not faithful. Instead, we must love them and show mercy to them so that, if possible, we may win them over to Christ. Otherwise, after they have helped lead us into our destiny, they may end up the same way Judas did.

The point I am making here though is that it is important to understand that not all those that we have on our staffs, boards, church memberships, various teams and circles of friends were planted in our lives by the Lord. Some are there because the Devil planted them in the night. The night speaks of things that are not yet seen, not yet revealed to us. But there is nothing hidden from the Father. So even though the Devil will plant things at night, and we are unaware, our Father (who neither sleeps nor slumbers) is watching. He knows those who are His and those who are not. He has not caused it, but He has allowed it.

In this parable, we are learning that if God removed the weeds from our businesses before time it could destroy the business as well. If weeds are removed from our churches before time, the people that God gave us to shepherd may be lost as well. So, we must be slow, extremely slow to deal with people that we consider weeds. If we deal with them outside of God's time we will also be destroyed in the process. Many times, the Lord deals with them without us ever having to interfere.

These are Jesus' definitions of weeds. They show us how dealing with weeds encompasses every area of our lives- overcoming the worries of this life, escaping the deceitfulness of riches, handling people well, dealing with unproductive habits, dealing with sin and many more.

100 Percent Fruitfulness

If these things are effectively dealt with in the gardens of our hearts, we will become a beautiful and fruitful well-watered garden. We will become like the kind of soil that gave back a 100% return on the seed that was planted. Let's take a deeper look at what 100% productivity looks like.

Observing the soils again in Jesus' parable we see that some ground produced no fruit (death) while some ground was 30% fruitful, some 60% fruitful and some 100% fruitful. The Lord gave Dr Bailey, founder of Zion Ministerial Institute, this interesting and yet challenging perspective about fruitfulness. *"Someone who is 60 percent fruitful can also be viewed as forty percent unfruitful. Someone who is 30 percent fruitful can also be viewed as 70 percent off the mark. Why? Because God created us in such a way that we can all get to a 100 percent fruitfulness. ALL OF US."* This includes you.

The soil that was 100% fruitful is the soil that dealt fully with weeds, all other soils didn't. So, an important question to ask yourself as you approach all of life's activities is, "What kind of soil would I like to be?" You have the capability to become the 100 % fruitful soil. But weeds will often stand in the way of that. Weeds cause us to settle for less than God's best for our lives; for less than what we were blessed with in Jesus Christ. If these weeds aren't dealt with fully, there is a danger looming. The greater danger of weeds.

The Greater Danger of Weeds

As we've already seen in the parable of the wheat and the weeds, **weeds come from the enemy.** Knowing that weeds come from the Devil gives us a glimpse into the greater danger that they pose. Imagine yourself in battle. Maybe you are William Wallace fighting for the freedom of your nation. One morning you wake up to find that a big breakfast has been prepared for you and delivered to your doorstep free of charge. When you ask the delivery person where the breakfast came from, they smile and say your enemy purchased it for you. What would you do with it? I'm sure like me, you wouldn't eat it under any circumstances. You would rather go hungry than eat a breakfast that has been given to you by your enemy. Well, it's the same with weeds. Jesus has given us a heads up by saying that every time we see something that can be defined as a weed in our lives, it is like a nice breakfast being served to you by your enemy. Don't eat it! There is no chance that it is good for you. If it's from your enemy it's definitely bad. It's not just bad, it's dangerous. It is designed to take you out of the fight. And you ought to deal with it quickly and wisely.

Jesus is teaching a particularly important lesson- the danger with weeds is not only how they reduce productivity. The greater danger of weeds is that they choke the plants to death. For the believer this means losing our faith and (without repentance) it means eternity in the fires of hell. That is the ULTIMATE danger of weeds. This doesn't just happen overnight and neither does it happen by accident. It begins with maybe just one dead area in our hearts. And, if we do not deal with this area, it leads to more dead areas in our hearts. Eventually this leads to a complete spiritual death - a falling away from the walk of faith. This is what this parable of the soils means when it talks about thorns stopping the ground from being fruitful. The ground had the ability to be fertile (otherwise the thorns wouldn't have been able to grow), but the weeds choke and eventually kill those seeds until there is more than just no fruit, there's no life either. When we realise the greater danger of weeds (death) we can appreciate the urgency of the need to deal with them. Dealing with weeds is, first of all, a matter of life and death before it is a matter of being more or less fruitful. In light of this important realisation, here are some reflection questions to help you and I get started on identifying the weeds in our lives as we conclude this section.

Conclusion

Now that we have defined weeds, we will turn our attention to dealing with them. As we do this, we will keep in mind the insight above from Dr Bailey. Even one percent less than 100% productivity is one percent less than what God intended for us. Do not settle for less than God's best for you. Let's conclude with some reflections.

<u>REFLECTION</u>

- Based on Jesus' standard of what a weed is (people, worries of this life and deceitfulness of wealth) what weeds have been misdiagnosed in my life?

  _____

  _____

  _____

  _____

- In what areas of my life am I led by worry instead of faith?

  _____

  _____

  _____

  _____

  _____

- In what areas of my life may I be deceived by the pleasure, delight, and glamour of riches?

  _____

  _____

  _____

  _____

  _____

- How is God challenging me to deal with difficult people (who might be weeds) in my life without trying to uproot them myself?

  _____

  _____

  _____

  _____

  _____

- In dealing with weeds in my life, what one thing can I do based on what I have learned today to help me increase my fruitfulness as a garden of the Lord?

  _____

  _____

  _____

  _____

  _____

SECTION II

WEEDS: HOW TO DEAL WITH THEM

INTRODUCTION

※

Understanding Helps us Work Smarter

True learning creates a hunger- a desire to work. It also gives us an understanding that causes us to want to go the extra mile- to work much harder. This desire and willingness to work hard is increased by the motivation that comes from seeing the fruitfulness of our efforts. This is why employers gladly send their employees to conferences, seminars, trainings, and other types of learning environments. The money and time invested into these is worth it because they help inspire a fresh willingness to not just get the work done but to get it done excellently. A similar thing happens with weeds. Learning about their qualities equips us to effectively deal with them. It gives us an understanding that helps us work smarter.

In light of this, we will now turn our attention to understanding the qualities of weeds. Most effective ways of dealing with weeds are linked to their qualities. As we observe each of them, we will learn the best way to deal with the weeds in our lives. It is true that we can often learn the spiritual things of life by first observing, studying and understanding the natural ones. This is what Paul meant when he said, *"seeing the visible makes us understand the invisible." (Romans 1:20 TPT).* Once we understand the characteristics of weeds, the strategy for dealing with them often becomes obvious.

As I learnt about weeds in the natural, I realised that it is not necessarily about having a new or more sophisticated strategy for productivity. It is more about learning to apply the common everyday life strategies that we have but with a new and better understanding of ourselves and how weeds work. We upgrade our ability to overcome weeds by increasing our understanding of their qualities. It is this understanding that I hope you gain in the next section. This understanding often leads to doing less, not more because what we are doing is that much more effective. One act done with understanding is often worth more than ten attempts done in ignorance. Understanding helps us work smarter, and inspiration helps us work harder. The result of these two (working harder and working smarter) is that we get better. We get better at being the person God created us to be- the garden He planted with his own hands.

We will learn about ourselves in a way that will motivate us to work on ourselves not out of obligation or duty but rather from a place of understanding and inspiration. The list of the qualities of weeds that we are going to look at in this section is not exhaustive. Far from it! I intentionally chose these three because they were the most helpful as I dealt with my own weeds. They were the most useful in helping me move forward in fruitfulness.

Wholeness, Completeness and Perfection

Another reason I chose these three qualities of weeds is because of the significance of what the number 3 symbolises Biblically- divine wholeness, completeness, and perfection. Most noteworthy figures and events in the Bible have the number 3 attached to them. This is a symbol of a Divine stamp of completion or fulfilment on the subject. Here are some examples from the Bible and from life showing the significance of the number 3:

- Three times Jesus asked Peter to feed His people after Peter's restoration
- Three people witnessed the transfiguration of Jesus.
- Three men hung from crosses at the crucifixion.
- Three angels are mentioned by name in the Bible
- Three parts to every human being- spirit, soul, and body
- Three ways that God is described, in the very beginning of the book of Revelation, as a Being *"which is, and which was, and which is to come" (Revelation 1:4 KJV).*

- Three segments of a day; morning, afternoon, and evening.
- Trinity; three "parts" to one God- Father, Son and Holy Spirit.

As you learn to deal with your weeds based on the three qualities we are going to explore, my hope is that the Lord brings you into wholeness, completeness, and perfection. I hope that the broken areas of your life are made whole. I hope that the information you glean here will fill and complete gaps that have stood in the way of you receiving the complete revelation of Christ. I hope that this book is a part of your journey in being perfected into the likeness of Christ.

Quality 1

---※---

Weeds Have Roots

CHAPTER 5

✳

Uprooting

*"Every plant that My Heavenly Father
has not planted will be pulled up by
its roots." (Matthew 15:13 NLT)*

*"Next to knowing God, the most important thing is
to know ourselves and to know what really is at the
bottom of our problems."
(Dr Paul G Caram)*

The Parking Lot Project

A few years ago, we decided to embark on a project to beautify the Community Centre where our church community gathers for services. There was a small tree positioned in the centre of what we wanted to turn into the driveway of the parking lot. There was no way of building around it so we decided to cut it down in order to make room for cars to drive in and out of the new parking lot with more ease. Though unspoken, one of the motivating factors for the decision may have been the fact that the tree looked so small that we didn't think it would be that big of a deal to cut it down. We estimated that we would be done in one or two hours and planned to then move on to a different phase of the beautification project.

In many ways this felt to us like a small side project that would pave the way for the main project. So, the work began.

As the work progressed, we encountered something that made us think that this tree may have been cut down before (probably more than once). We noticed that its roots were much deeper than we expected for a tree of its size. The roots were so deep that it took us the better part of one and a half days to fully remove the tree from the site. What initially started off as a side project eventually became the main project and for some of the team members it became the only project. Where our eyes saw a small tree, we were actually dealing with very deep and well-developed root systems. Uprooting them ended up costing us more time than we had budgeted, required more effort than we had expected and ultimately this was a much bigger project than what it looked like initially. When dealing with weeds it is important to understand that what you and I see on the surface is not the real problem. The real problem lies underneath the surface. I learnt this lesson the hard way through this project.

Looking Beneath the Surface

This experience taught me a priceless lesson. It gave me a picture of how we, as believers, often cut down weeds from our lives without ever touching the roots giving life to those weeds. We do this by focusing on modifying our behaviour without understanding and uprooting the root systems that are giving the weeds life. We concern ourselves with what can be seen but leave the root system intact. As a result, it is not long before the weed grows back. However, in growing back the weed looks like it is a minor problem, and we don't think it is that big of a deal. It doesn't seem like it's a big problem because, just like that tree that looked small to us, this weed in our lives has been cut down many times and is in the process of regrowing. Because its root system has never been touched, the roots go so deep that it's only a matter of time before it completely destroys the house (our lives).

I love the words of Jesus in the book of John when He said, ***"Look beneath the surface so you can judge correctly." (John 7:24 NLT).*** Because we often deal with what is on the surface while ignoring the root system, even the very small issues in our lives can be a sign that there is a big problem. There might be a root system that needs to be uprooted before it overwhelms and kills us. When dealing with our weeds, we ought to look closely at the small things- the recurring struggles and patterns that keep coming back after we've tried to deal with them. We need to get skilled at looking beneath the surface of our lives and our organisations so that we can judge correctly. We need to pay attention to our 'slips of the tongue.' To effectively deal with our weeds -to uproot them - we must be correct, not just sincere. The reason this matters is because, in the same way that a root in nature continues to be active underground even after the tree has been cut off, a root in our hearts continues to grow and be active in our lives until it is completely uprooted. So, if there is a weed, it is a matter of urgency that we uproot it. If not, it keeps going deeper and deeper regardless of our efforts to cut off its tree.

Over Time, Not Overnight

The reason this error is repeated so often is **because focusing on the surface gives us the perception of immediate results and we live in a world that loves immediate results.** We live in a world that keeps feeding us the thinking, "Under the right conditions you can get whatever you desire in an instant." Here are a few examples that I could think of:

- *If you want to go on a date, just swipe right on a phone app and "Voila!" you have a date.*
- *If you want to go shopping, just log into you amazon account from the comfort of your couch and you are instantly in-store and shopping*
- *If you want popcorn, just throw a bag into the microwave and you'll have it in under 3 minutes.*
- *If you want to make a difference, just sponsor a child in Africa for thirty dollars and you will make a difference instantly.*
- *If you want to connect with your friends, send an instant message to them and you'll get a response from them immediately (your app will even help you see that they are typing a response while you wait).*
- *If you want to drive just … (well that one still requires that you get into a car and actually learn to do it over time).*

So, we can see that most things in life are being reduced to instant production. This thinking sometimes causes us to approach God expecting Him to give us the things that our hearts yearn for in an instant. We think that if it is taking long, it means something is wrong. Unfortunately, when it comes to weeds, this is a poor approach. As exciting as those immediate results are, it doesn't take long for the weeds to grow back. Over time, this leads to an up and down cycle of excitement- discouragement less excitement-more discouragement even less excitement-disillusionment even less excitement- and finally depression. I've tried to illustrate the cycle using the diagram below:

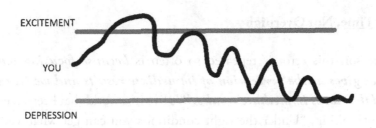

This up and down cycle in how we feel about life, others, ourselves and even God is a result of treating the symptoms of weeds without ever dealing with their roots. It is like giving headache tablets to someone who is suffering from malaria because you want to give them instant relief from the pain. The effect of those tablets may be to give quick relief from the symptoms caused by the malaria parasite. However, this relief will only last for a short while. Before long, the headache comes back, and oftentimes it comes back stronger with further complications. Ultimately, if the malaria is not properly treated, this will lead to death.

A remarkably similar thing tends to happen when we are trying to deal with weeds in our lives. We deal with the symptoms of the weed trying to get a quick solution. Instead, like it is with the malaria headache, we progressively get worse. As we get worse while we are doing all we can to get better, our self-esteem is affected. We begin to conclude that there must be something wrong with us. Say, for example, you've been trying to overcome a drug problem for a long time. You've taken the medication prescribed to you by the doctors, you've gone to rehab, and you've found an accountability partner, but you keep relapsing and maybe even getting worse. How would this make you feel? Is it fair to assume that this may begin to affect your self-esteem? Is it likely that those around you may begin to think that you are not serious about changing (and yet you are)? Yes, it is.

This is a classic example of the effect of dealing with the symptoms of the weed without ever touching its roots. In this example it may just be that the drug problem is related to the abuse you encountered as a child. When you finally properly deal with it and remove the root of rejection that this may have planted in you, you will find long lasting success in dealing with the drug problem. With drugs, as with many other challenges we face in adulthood, the root is often found in our early developmental stages, especially our childhood. These roots continue to develop as we grow into our adulthood and, if left undealt with, they will never stop producing thorns that continuously choke the life out of the good plants that we are trying to grow in our lives. This is part of the reason weeds often grow faster than the seeds of God's Word planted in our hearts later in life. It is because the weeds already had roots in the ground. And because those roots run deep, they give the weeds a head start. The result is that the weeds outgrow the plants which are still in the initial stages of building their root system.

Getting to the root of weeds takes time so we need to shift our mindset from the thinking of 'instant everything.' We need a mindset shift back to the times when you would watch one episode per week of your favourite show and then have to wait a solid seven days before watching another one; to the days when you couldn't get in touch with your parents at any moment of the day- you had to wait for them to get home so you can call them on the landline telephone in the house; to the times when popcorn didn't come from the microwave- it needed a pot and cooking oil and you had to sit by the stove listening for the perfect time to remove it from the stove without burning it (nobody likes chargrilled popcorn). Without this shift in thinking, dealing with weeds becomes another disappointing phase in our lives that we dismiss as being unfruitful because the results didn't come in an instant.

I would like to encourage you and let you know that though this road is long and takes more time than we prefer, it is worth it. I want you to know that even though the changes that I made in my life didn't bear fruit overnight, they did eventually bear fruit. What didn't happen overnight, eventually happened over time, and, when that fruit started coming, it was so sweet it made the time taken dealing with weeds worth it. God wants you and I to be his, *"trees of righteousness [strong and magnificent, distinguished for integrity, justice, and right standing with God]." Isaiah 61:3b AMP.* You and I start off as green shoots like the message translation's expression of this same verse. But it is the Lord's desire and design for us to become strong, magnificent, distinguished people of integrity, justice and right standing with God (righteousness). This happens over time; it does not happen overnight.

Changing My Mindset

However, there is something that can happen overnight. In fact, it can happen in an instant. In an instant, in this instant, you and I can choose. We can choose to stop focusing on just changing the result of the weeds. We can choose to start focusing on identifying the roots that feed them. We can choose to change our mindset from seeking superficial immediate results to committing to a process that will produce lasting results. We can choose to not settle for the appearance of health but rather working to be truly healthy. In our organisations, we can choose to not be given to appearance management and choose rather to focus on going deeper when addressing issues. This is how we apply the understanding of this simple but important quality of weeds; weeds have roots. Here are some examples of how we can apply this understanding.

*Say you have an anger issue that causes you to lash out. You might be tempted to avoid people or learn how to fake smiles, so you do not show people how you are truly feeling on the inside. Instead, you can choose to engage in counselling that might take months or spend some time in prayer over a long period and ask God to reveal why you are angry and help you deal with it. Prayer and counselling might take longer but they are more likely to help you get to the roots of your anger issue.

*You have a new car. This car makes you feel more important because those around you have less expensive cars. You could pretend to be humble by offering people free rides while harbouring pride on the inside. Or you could be vulnerable to a mentor and ask him to help you get to the root of how you view yourself and your possessions. This may take longer but it is more likely to help you overcome the pride and insecurity that you are dealing with.

*At school there is a subject that is giving you trouble. You just can't understand what the teacher is teaching. You could copy your friend's assignment so that you do not fail and have to repeat the class. Or you could ask for extra lessons from the teacher. They will cost you more time and might even cost you financially but in the end you would have solved your real problem of not understanding the subject.

These are some everyday examples of how we can practically change our mindset from focusing on immediate results to dealing with the roots of our weeds. This is how we begin the journey to becoming truly free.

Becoming Truly Free

John 8:36 GNT, "If the Son sets you free, then you will be really free." To be really (truly, completely, genuinely) free is only possible when I am free of the roots of my bondage not just the behaviour that was manifesting as the bondage. Then I am free from the power of sin (deliverance), not just the penalty of sin (forgiveness). So, as you've been identifying the weeds in your life, remember, there is a root for every tree. Before there was ever a weed a seed was planted. The most fruitful question to ask when I find behaviours that keep choking the life of Christ in me is, "What is the root cause of this behaviour, feeling, attitude etc?" God, in His mercy, wants to help us identify our roots so we can deal with them.

"I am the Root and the Offspring of David," (Revelations 22:16NIV). Jesus identified himself as the Root because when we invite Him to come into our lives, He comes in to replace the roots that have kept us in bondage. In every heart where Jesus is received as King, He becomes the Root out of which that life produces fruit. The name David means

beloved and therefore in declaring that He is the "root of David,' Jesus is saying that He desires to make us into God's beloved garden- one where He comes in and walks about and just enjoys its beauty. I can relate with this because one of my favourite things to do is to sit and enjoy a garden. Some of my most intimate times with God have been in gardens. Some of the messages I've preached in church were given to me by the Lord in a garden. As I have already mentioned, there are many thoughts in this book that came to me in the garden. That is the kind of garden God desires you and I to be. And Jesus is the root that makes that possible.

Jesus leads us on this journey of dealing with our weeds in the same way that a good shepherd leads his sheep. In His kindness, He helps us deal with one thing at a time. And, every time He reveals something, He has already provided the grace for us to deal with it. Our calling is to trust Him and obey. Armed with this new mindset of getting to the root of our weeds there is a key practice that we must incorporate into our lives, RETRACING OUR STEPS. Let's look at this practice in detail in the next chapter.

CHAPTER 6

※

Retracing Our Steps

In order to fully understand a matter,
we need to go back to where it began.

Going Back to The Beginning

In life, the root of every issue is linked to how it began. If you are dealing with a weed, it is immensely helpful to retrace your steps to the time when it started growing in your life. Picture what was going on in your life at that moment. Try to identify major events in your life around that time. For example, if you are dealing with an addiction and, when you retrace your steps, you realise that there was a death in the family around the time you began this behaviour, it may be that your addiction is linked to some unresolved grief. Grief counselling could help you get to the root of it. If, on the other hand, you find that this behaviour began when you were in the middle of a strenuous season preparing for exams, the root of the addiction may be related to unhealthy patterns of dealing with stress. These are only examples of course, but I hope you get the picture. The key to identifying the roots of weeds in your life is to retrace your steps. Retracing your steps can be done personally as well as with the help of others (communally).

Retracing Our Steps Personally

Retracing our steps personally happens best when we take some time to be alone. We do this by separating ourselves from the busyness of life and being by ourselves before the Lord. In that quietness, we gain an opportunity to reflect on patterns in our life in ways that we can't do in the noise of everyday life. The more often we take this kind of time to reflect, the less likely it is that we will be overcome by weeds. We will be able to catch them early and deal with them quickly. Jesus had a similar practice while he lived on the earth. Luke tells us that Jesus frequently *"would go away to lonely places, where he prayed." Luke 5:16 GNT* This practice is preventative. It is essential in preventing weeds from growing in our garden. When done well, it stops us from being reactive in our process of dealing with weeds. This is because it stops weeds from taking roots in our hearts in the first place. We do not always have to wait until we have had a meltdown for us to begin trying to understand what is going on in our hearts. The wiser thing to do is, like Jesus, frequently have time when we are by ourselves. In those times, we can present ourselves to the Lord in prayer and deal with things that He points out in our hearts.

When we are alone, things that are being drowned out by the noise are given a chance to be heard. This is what happens during the night-time; the silence allows us to hear the clocks ticking. The silence doesn't cause the clock to tick. The clock had been ticking all day, but it was being drowned out by the noise. What could you learn from a few moments of being alone with God today? How about a few moments of being alone with God every day? One of the biggest values of a daily devotional time is its ability to help us identify weeds early. These weeds have the potential to take root and cause damage if left undealt with today. It is helpful to retrace our steps while things are still fresh and while there still aren't yet many steps to retrace. This is because roots are often related to how things began. The book of Ephesians teaches us, *"Be angry and do not sin; do not let the sun go down on your anger" Ephesians 2:26 NRSV.* Why should I not let the sun go down in my anger? Because, when I do, I am allowing a weed to take root in my heart. Before the sun goes down, I need to have dealt with it so that I prevent it from planting itself in my heart in the night-time since weeds are planted by our enemy in the night as we see in *Matthew 13;25 ESV, "while his men were sleeping, his enemy came and sowed weeds"* It is essential to reflect on our day.

There is a literal interpretation of these verses as well as a spiritual interpretation. The literal interpretation is that we must not go to bed with offences that we haven't released. The spiritual interpretation is that while we are still alert to certain things that have gone on in our lives- our marriages, our businesses, and other areas- we ought to deal with them quickly before they are drowned out by other cares, and we become 'asleep to them' as it were. If we do not, we have given the enemy an opportunity to plant a weed in our heart. Everything that is swept under the carpet has been given free licence to plant itself in my heart. So, what is the solution? Sweep it out of the house while you are still alert to it. Ask your wife for forgiveness while you are still alert to the fact that you hurt her feelings by the way you spoke to her when the visitors were around. Sit down and debrief how the service went while you are still alert to some of the mistakes that you want your team to be careful not to repeat. Call in your employees and have a quick chat reminding them about the vision of the company while your observation of their disrespectful behaviour towards a customer is still fresh in your mind. Parents, explain to your children what was going on in the movie that you just watched together while that disturbing scene is still fresh on their minds. When we delay and put off addressing these simple issues, we are giving the enemy a space to plant lies in our hearts. Those lies become roots that feed the weeds we eventually find ourselves dealing with later in life.

If we do not delay, we ultimately do less. This is the secret to becoming more fruitful through less not more- learning to do things at the right time or in other words, within the God-given window of opportunity to deal with it. In a farm the timing for when certain tasks should be done is extremely specific based on the seasons of the year. God is giving us the opportunity to do certain things like plant seed, harvest crops, etc. When that time is respected and things are done according to their times, the farm is fruitful, and the work is significant. But when things are done late, the work that already requires significant effort becomes stressful. It takes more effort to do it and the fruit produced is less. The key is to learn the principle of doing what needs to be done today, today. *"There is a time for everything, and a season for every activity under the heavens."*

Ecclesiastes 3: 1 NIV. So let us take the opportunity God has given us today to retrace our steps and remove weeds before they take root in our hearts and become a bigger problem.

Retracing Our Steps Communally

One morning, while Zinty and I were reading a marriage book, we came to a part of the book that really spoke to her. Because of this she began to speak passionately about what she was learning. This caused her to become slightly animated and raise her voice a little bit almost as if she was getting angry. While all this was happening, I began to feel uncomfortable. Her passion and emotion unsettled me. Even though this wasn't pointed at me in a negative way I just couldn't shake off the feeling of discomfort that it was giving me. I was so uncomfortable I wanted her to stop. Come to think of it, this wasn't the first time I had felt this way. I would often feel extremely uncomfortable whenever something like this happened. Whether it was Zinty crying or having a passionate discussion with her siblings. So, that day, instead of hiding I decided to take a risk and tell her exactly what I was feeling. I said, "You know what, even though you are not upset at me in any way and this show of passion is meant to be positive, I'm uncomfortable with it. I don't know why but that's where I'm at."

Without flinching, Zinty responded as only Zinty can, "I know you are uncomfortable, and I can tell you why." I tensed up a little bit and began to feel myself become slightly defensive. Zinty, excited by the opportunity she had to show me how much she knew and understood me, went on (one of Zinty's love languages is figuring people out :-)). *"You grew up in a home where the only times that passion was shown was when something wrong was happening. As a result, every time you see passion in our home you fear that something wrong is happening."* Once she got done speaking, I laughed aloud. Half of this laugh was because of how correct she was. She was spot on. The other half was because my tension had turned to relief as I realised that Zinty was spot on with her observation. As difficult as it was, I made the decision to soften my heart to what she was saying. I knew that if I didn't allow offence to cloud my judgement, there was so much I could gain from what she had just said.

In my upbringing, I often saw my parents and relatives be passionate when there was a misunderstanding, a disagreement or a fight (some of them physical). It was not common to see those same levels of passion when something positive was happening. This planted a root in my heart that caused me to fear heightened emotions and passionate expressions. And without realising it, every time my wife became passionate, I feared that something was wrong. Oftentimes my biggest fear was that she was upset with me and because of that I would withdraw. That is why I laughed, because she was spot on in her assessment. She helped me get to the root of why I had this fear of heightened emotions and passion in our marriage and in our home. Realising this brought so much relief, not because I was completely healed of this fear but simply because I knew why. Knowing this in the community of my marriage relationship meant that I was sharing it with someone- someone who loved me and wanted me to get better. It really is true that a problem known is a problem half-solved

As we can see from my experience, retracing our steps is also done with the help of others. Every human being has a history. And whether we like it or not, our history affects us in some way. Parts of our history affect us positively. An example of this is a decent financial inheritance left for you by parents who were good stewards of their finances. However, other parts of our history affect us negatively. An example could be having parents who didn't believe in educating women. This could result in missed job opportunities because you do not possess the required education. Because of this you could end up battling with certain weeds that others are not battling with. Knowing about this history will help you resolve and uproot weeds that you are dealing with from a better vantage point.

Ilima

So, who in your life can you share your problems with? Who can you be transparent with about the real you? Who knows you enough to help you get to the root of your weeds? My hope is that you do not try and get better alone, because the moment we isolate ourselves we get worse. We become easy prey for the enemy in the same way that lions always target the antelopes that are separate from the herd. ***"He who isolates himself pursues selfish desires; he rebels against all sound judgment."***

(Proverbs 18:1 Berean Study Bible). It is exceedingly difficult to make sound judgements when you are isolated. That is why aeroplanes rarely fly without two pilots. That is why there is no army made up of one person. And that is why right at the beginning of creation God looked at Adam (even before the fall) and said, *"It is not good for the man to be alone. I will make him a helper suitable for him" Genesis 2:18 NIV*

If isolation wasn't good even before the fall, it means that needing help from others is not a weakness to be frowned upon. Needing help from others is not a result of the fall. It is not a part of the curse. Rather, it is a part of the way God created us, a part of the image of God present in us. Everything God created exists in community and everything God created thrives in community. Trees are known to grow better when they are planted around other trees. Animals often travel in herds and hunt in packs. Even God Himself exists in the community of the Trinity and He created us in His image. This means we are at our best as God's creation when we are in community. And this principle extends to our weeds. We need the community around us to help us remove weeds from inside us.

I was born in Zimbabwe and my family is a part of the Ndebele tribe. The Ndebeles used to support themselves primarily through planting crops (like maize and sorghum) and rearing livestock (like cows and goats). The fields on which they planted maize and sorghum had to be very big if they were to harvest enough crops to sustain themselves through the year. They were so big, in fact, that most families were not able to weed them on their own. The solution that they produced for weeding their fields was to invite the community to join hands and come and help them weed their fields. They called these events "Ilima" which means "the day of weeding." On this day, every able-bodied member of the community would drop what they were doing, come to one person's home at the break of dawn and help them remove weeds from their maize field until they are done. In return, the owner of the field would give them a meal (and oftentimes free beer as well).

This practice was so effective that the Ndebeles, for a long time in their history, were able to feed themselves from their fields without the use of modern machinery. This practice is so effective it is still being practiced in some places today. Many of the people who participated in this practice were able to harvest enough grain to last them until the next season of planting. If you asked most farmers, they'll tell you that for someone to harvest that much without using modern machinery is nothing short of a miracle. However, for me, the bigger miracle is not how much they harvest, it is the fact that they harvest it without being overwhelmed. They harvest so much while having fun in the process. Because they are in community the work becomes a joy not a burden and this results in a bigger harvest. The Ndebeles, without realising it, are putting into practice the principle that God introduced to us in the garden of Eden by choosing not to do their lives and their work alone. They bring helpers around them who are suitable to help them get the job done.

The 'ilima' practice gives us a perfect illustration of the power that is found in retracing our steps in community as we deal with our weeds. Dealing with weeds is a team effort. We need others. There are many diverse types of gardens but there is one thing that is common to all of them- with the help of others, they become easier to manage. It is the same with the spiritual garden of our lives and our hearts. We need the help of others, whether it be pastors, mentors, parents, coaches, friends, etc. On our own we easily get tired, discouraged, and lose heart. On our own, we almost always settle for good enough when God is calling us to greatness. This is why in order to bring out the greatness that is in you and me, we need the help of others in the faith. This means we must be willing to go through the discomfort of transparency, accountability, submission, correction, and discipline. This is how we get to the root of all the weeds stunting the growth that we desire to see in our careers, in our ministries, in our marriages and in every other area where God has called us to be fruitful.

It is encouraging to know that, with the help of others, we can deal with almost anything. Burdens that are heavy begin to feel lighter. Like the English writer John Heywood said, *"Many hands make light work."* So, if you feel burdened when you look at the state of your life right now, it is possible that the issue may not be the number of weeds but rather the number of people helping you deal with them. You and I were not made to do life without help. Without the help of others, it doesn't take long to get overwhelmed by our weeds. It is good to deal with the roots of your weeds around the encouragement that comes from others who have dealt with the same things before. It is empowering to see those who love and care for us helping us carry our burdens even if opening up to them might be scary at first.

As you retrace your steps, let me ask you this simple question, "Who is helping you do this?" It is not a sign of weakness to need help from your spouse, from your parents or children (yes, parents, children can help us retrace our steps. Remember that they have been with you ever since they were born), from our spiritual leaders and, leaders, from those that we are leading. In the same way that farmers don't just plant crops haphazardly, the Lord in His mercy handpicks the people around us so that we can be empowered to live a fruitful life. Farmers choose the perfect spacing for their crops and oftentimes they will even plant specific herbs and trees around those crops to keep away harmful insects that could negatively affect productivity. Our master farmer, God Himself, has chosen for us the community that we need to be most fruitful in our lives. We need meekness in order to accept this community and learn from it even if it may not always be under the circumstances that we prefer. In the same way that plants need to be in community in the garden in order to flourish, we need to be in community to thrive.

The Truth Helps, Even If It Hurts At First

There is a common misconception that when we grow up and progress in life, we cease to be able to learn from those behind us or those who haven't yet attained the same levels of success that we have. But the truth is that we can learn something from just about anybody. Galileo Galilei, an Italian astronomer & physicist once famously said, *"I have never met a man so ignorant that I couldn't learn something from him."* Now think about that for a moment; an astronomer or physicist is, by any standard, a highly educated person. And yet Galilei was both an astronomer and physicist. He surely must have been a highly accomplished and educated person and yet he says of himself that he could learn something from just about any human being. If even an astronomer realises their need for help from people of all walks of life, I know that we can all learn something from the people that the Lord has handpicked to be around us. Moses led the people of God through many miraculous experiences, but he learned a valuable lesson from his father-in-law who taught him how to manage his time and the affairs of the nation of Israel. Even though his father-in-law could not match the level of revelation that Moses had been given, it is clear that the wisdom that he had (and gave) in the area of time management was helpful to Moses. It helped him become a better leader to God's people.

Yet, as I observed how this advice came about, it could have been easy for Moses to have trouble receiving it. He could even have been hurt by some of what his father-in-law observed and shared. After observing how he worked, Moses' father-in-law remarked, ***"You are not doing it the right way. You will wear yourself out and these people as well. This is too much for you to do alone." Exodus 18:18 GNB.*** Put yourself in Moses's shoes for a second. You've been working all day doing what you believe is God's work. You have given your best and are now tired and ready for some rest. Then your father-in-law comes to you after the day has ended and says something like that. How would you feel? Is it possible that it might hurt a little? Or maybe a lot? Well, that is the challenge that truth brings us. The truth helps, even if it hurts at first.

Oftentimes when someone gets to the root of something going on in our hearts, it hurts before it helps us. This is what people are trying to say when they say the 'truth hurts.' I felt a little of this when Zinty was telling me her observation about my fear of emotion and passion. As she shared her observation, my initial feeling was to resist her and argue. It was like she unmasked me; like she exposed me a little bit. And in that moment of feeling naked I had a choice to make; either I was going to humble myself and learn or I was going to exalt myself and rebel against what she was saying. This is why isolation is bad. When people get close to us, they see more. When they are far away, they see less and therefore can't objectively challenge us in areas where we need to grow. Isolation will often make us think we are better off than we truly are because we aren't being challenged in areas of our weaknesses and sinfulness.

The challenge that is truly a blessing is the one that comes from someone who knows enough to 'hit the nail on the head' when confronting us on our sinfulness. Proverbs teaches us that, ***"Wounds from a sincere friend are better than many kisses from an enemy." Proverbs 27:6 NLT*** I hope you have the kind of friends that love you enough to wound you to health. Modern culture is quite individualistic. This works against us when it comes to dealing with weeds. This is because we find that even though we have a lot of people around us, we aren't truly known by many of them if any. This makes getting to the root of our weeds a lot harder and oftentimes, I believe, impossible. The individualistic nature of culture is caused by the fact that the closer people are to us the more vulnerable we become to them. This vulnerability works in two ways. We can either be loved and cherished by those who are closest to us, or we can be wounded and betrayed by them. The risk of being wounded often causes people to prefer isolation over community.

I would like to encourage you to consider the alternative. Consider how, because of being vulnerable, you might see things that you would never have seen before. You might be healed and delivered in areas where you have struggled to overcome for a long time. That and many other reasons, in my opinion, makes being vulnerable worth it, in spite of the risk. When Zinty spoke to me, she wounded me a little, but she helped me too. She spoke about my family in a rather negative way, and I could have taken offence. However, in the end, I cherished her words because they were sincere. I also cherished them because they weren't just sincere, they were helpful. They left me a better person.

I remember another time when Zinty politely said, "Lue, you are a great preacher, but you are an average singer. It will be better for you to focus on preaching and if you need a song to be sung ask me or the worship team to help." In that moment I experienced Proverbs 27:6 again. Did I prefer hearing that I am an average singer? No. Did it help me to be told to my face that my singing was not helpful to me or those listening? Yes. In wounding me slightly with her direct comment of my preaching and singing combo it is likely that she saved me from a lot of embarrassment when I listened back to the recording of my singing. But she didn't just do that; she also saved the congregation from suffering through less than preferred renditions of my favourite worship songs. This shows that there is another benefit to being vulnerable. It helps those who are around us. If we allow ourselves to be vulnerable and receive 'difficult to receive feedback' we create environments that are life-giving for those who are listening to us as preachers, those who are following us as leaders, those who look up to us as parents and those who interact with us in general life settings as people.

So, let's embrace this understanding that not everyone who calls us out is out to get us. Some of them are sincere enough to risk wounding us so they can help us. Getting good at retracing your steps so that you can uproot weeds in your life requires you to get good at allowing people into your life. It requires that you allow them to come close enough that they could wound you, because if they are sincere, their wounds can be trusted. Their wounds will leave you better and will result in all those that you touch being blessed. *"Faithful are the wounds of a friend." Proverbs 27: 6 NKJV.* They remove weeds that could have eventually cost us our souls.

Community Means Many Not Few

The roots that give life to our weeds are not only from our childhood. They are also from before our childhood. This is the reason we need the help of others in retracing our steps. Examples of people who can help us retrace our steps are parents, friends (especially those we've had for a long time), spouses, and others. Each of these people have a unique perspective of our lives because of two things.

1. They have been a part of it.
2. They see it from a uniquely different angle- different from us and different from others too!

When these perspectives are gathered, we get a clearer picture of what we are dealing with. The Bible teaches us that *"Our knowledge is partial and incomplete" 1 Corinthians 13:9 NLT.* Each one of us sees only a part of the whole picture. And when those parts are put together, we see clearly. We are safe when we have a multitude of counsellors because we need a multitude of them in order to clearly identify the roots that we are dealing with. It is unsafe to rely on one or two perspectives because when that person misses it, they will lead you astray as well. It is also unsafe to rely on my perspective alone because as convincing as it may be, it is only a part of the whole picture. It is not the whole picture.

The solution, like Proverbs teaches us, is to have a multitude of counsellors. The dictionary defines the word multitude as, 'a vast number of people.' The Bible is teaching us that we learn not from a select few, but from, 'a vast number of people.' Not all these people are close confidants or associates; otherwise, that could lead us into confusion. However, just because someone is not a close confidant or an associate it doesn't mean that I cannot learn or benefit from them. If someone has a different perspective on an issue, one that I don't have, then it makes sense that I can learn something from them- even if it hurts, even if it leaves me feeling naked, even if there is only one grain of truth in what they are saying- that is one more grain than I currently have. And, if it is true, then it is something that I can benefit from as I try to get to the root of my weeds.

Oftentimes, I've found that when people give us advice there is a part of what they say that is true and there is another part of what they say that is unhelpful. This is because in the same way that I see in part, they also see in part. The result of this is that every time someone speaks, we must learn to take what is helpful and discard what isn't. Another way of saying it is that we need to *"eat the meat and spit out the bones."* This dynamic of how advice is often part helpful and part unhelpful is another reason why some people choose to isolate themselves completely and others choose to listen only to a select few. But true wisdom is to have a multitude of counsellors and take what is helpful while discarding what isn't. Even though this approach is more challenging, it proves to be safer and more fruitful in the end.

When uprooting weeds in a natural garden there is no way around the messiness of the process. Our clothes get muddy, our hands get muddy and even the plants that we are trying to nurture will have some mud on them. This is a picture of what community is like. It is messy. It makes us better but not before we have had some mud on our clothes. Do not let the mess distract you from the progress you are making. Some of your advisors won't be kind but that doesn't mean they aren't helpful. As you retrace your steps you will come upon some unexpected stuff to deal with but that doesn't mean you aren't making progress. I remember one day when the Lord spoke to my heart and said, ***"Just because something isn't working out the way you expected, it doesn't mean that it isn't working out."*** I would like to pass on that thought to you as you retrace your steps. You will encounter the unexpected, maybe even the unwanted but, "just because the journey doesn't lead you where you expected, it doesn't mean that you aren't making substantial progress." Have the courage to keep going even when you realise that you have more work to do than you initially estimated. The journey of dealing with weeds is about progress.

It's not about getting what we expected. In many instances holding on to our preconceived ideas and expectations keeps us from making true progress. The secret is to hold our expectations loosely enough to be able to let them go when they begin standing in the way of the goal of dealing with weeds, fruitfulness.

Of course, as it is with anything that is good, true, or helpful, retracing our steps can also be taken too far. So, as we conclude this chapter, let me caution us to not take this too far and end up trying to find a root in every small occurrence in our lives. There are some things that the Lord has chosen not to reveal to us at this time. He does this because of His mercy (the highest revelation of God is mercy). Everything that He chooses to do and not do, show, and not show is motivated by his mercy. *"The Lord is merciful and gracious, slow to anger, and plenteous in mercy." Psalm 103:8 KJV.* In due season we will know what we need to know. In the meantime, let us learn to retrace our steps without taking this good and helpful practice too far and in the process turning it into something toxic in our lives.

Conclusion

Retracing our steps personally and communally gives us a solid foundation for identifying the weeds we need to uproot. Doing one without the other causes us to be unbalanced. If we focus on retracing our steps personally and neglect doing it in community, we isolate ourselves. If we focus on retracing our steps in community but neglect doing it personally, we may become overwhelmed while starving ourselves of the light that comes from hearing the Holy Spirit's still, small voice; a voice that is often heard in the silence. Doing these two practices together with the right balance keeps us on the path of righteousness that God marked out for us. Overtime, not overnight, we will win our battle against weeds that are fighting against our souls.

Reflection Questions

- In what area am I seeking immediate results by modifying my behaviour without having first gotten to the root of the matter?

  _____

  _____

  _____

  _____

  _____

- How can I retrace my steps in this area?

  _____

  _____

  _____

  _____

  _____

- Who are some of the people in my life that can help me retrace my steps?

  _____

  _____

  _____

  _____

- In dealing with weeds in my life, what else can I do based on what I have learned today to help me increase my fruitfulness as a garden of the Lord?

  _____

  _____

  _____

  _____

  _____

- As we conclude, let me encourage you to take a few minutes to pause and welcome the input and leading of the Holy Spirit in this area.

_____

_____

_____

_____

_____

Quality 2

———————— ✳ ————————

Weeds Vary

CHAPTER 7

✳

Three Kinds of Weeds

*"'Do not mate different kinds of animals.
"'Do not plant your field with two kinds of
seed. "'Do not wear clothing woven of two
kinds of material."- Leviticus 19:19b NIV*

*When we recognise the unique differences in our
enemies, we are one step closer to victory. When
we fail to recognise the unique differences in our
enemies, we have taken one step towards defeat.*

One Word, Many Kinds

In farming and agriculture, it doesn't take long to realise that even though
one word is used to describe them, weeds have very distinct differences. As
I have taken the time to study weeds and how they affect plant life, I have
learned that there are principally three types of weeds: annual, biennial and
perennial weeds. The annual types of weeds have an average lifespan of a
year while the biennial type of weeds last an average of two years. The third
type, the perennial, is the most challenging to handle as it has been found
to return every year. It is known to produce long tap roots as well as seeds.

As we look at this natural definition of weeds, I would like to share three distinct kinds of weeds that we have to deal with in our lives (remember, nature always gives us a picture of what is spiritual).

1. The **annual weeds** speak of those things in our lives that we can deal with mostly on our own and usually after just one attempt.
2. The **biennial weeds** speak of those things in our lives that are dealt with over a longer period and require that we engage the help of community.
3. The **perennial weeds** are the kinds of weeds that we must continually fight until we meet Jesus face to face.

We can learn a lot about how we operate as humans from this research. In looking back over my life and the lives of others, I have observed that there are some things that I dealt with once and they were gone. With the benefit of hindsight, I can look back on those struggles and say that they seem like annual weeds to me. Then there are other struggles that I dealt with and eventually overcame. However, the victory did not come overnight, it came overtime. It took lots of prayer and even help from others to eventually overcome. These weeds seem like a biennial kind of weed to me because I couldn't overcome them on my own and I didn't overcome them overnight. This lesson is not new. We see this principle spoken of in the Bible when it says, **"Two are better than one, because they have a good return for their labour: If either of them falls down, one can help the other up. But pity anyone who falls and has no one to help them up." Ecclesiastes 4:9-10 NIV.** This principle applies to weeds as well. We spoke about this regarding retracing our steps communally in the previous chapter. It applies to biennial weeds as well. There are some things in our lives that can't be defeated in isolation. So, it is key for us to learn not to do spiritual warfare solo.

Perennial weeds are the kind of struggles that we will fight daily until the day we see Jesus. We will find that we seem to deal with these weeds every day. The ongoing temptation to be prideful is an example of a perennial weed. Those who think they have completely dealt with pride once and for all are the most susceptible to it. Why? It's a perennial weed. We fight it daily. We check our motives in every situation being careful to make sure we are free from the sin that so easily entangles. We never think and behave like we are completely safe from it because when we think we are strong we might find ourselves falling.

Examples from Scripture

We see an example of dealing with perennial weeds from Paul's instruction to us about the ongoing temptation to be prideful. He said, **"If you think you are standing strong, be careful not to fall." 1 Corinthians 10:12 NLT.** The moment we think we are strong, and we are past the temptation to be prideful is the point at which we are most vulnerable to falling into pride. Pride is a part of our sinful nature and is not something we can deal with once and be done with. It's also not just something we can cast out when doing spiritual warfare. It must be dealt with daily right up until we finish our earthly race.

The sin of lying on the other hand is something the Bible tells us to "strip off." **"Don't lie to each other, for you have stripped off your old sinful nature" Colossians 3:9 NLT.** This sounds to me like an annual weed. One where we can, by the grace of God, decide today to stop doing something and begin to immediately see results tomorrow. It doesn't mean we might not trip, fall, and need to pick ourselves up again. However, it does mean that we can be free from it in a more immediate manner than we are with the temptation of being prideful. Now that we have the nature of Jesus Christ in us, we possess the ability to overcome it by an act of our will.

A biennial sin is one where we will need the help of community to overcome. It is one where we can't just decide and be completely free from it by ourselves. I believe this is why James said, **"Therefore confess your sins to each other."** Why must we do this? Because we can then, **"pray for each other so that you may be healed. The prayer of a righteous person is powerful and effective" James 5:16 CSB.** So, let us not try to deal with a biennial weed using an annual weed strategy. When it comes to biennial weeds it takes two to deal with them. There are some weeds that will never be uprooted if we try to approach them solo. An example is sexual sins and sins having to do with financial integrity. These sins require that we be accountable to and supported by others as we choose to walk in victory over them.

Defining the Weeds in Your Life

As you have read and seen how weeds are different- perennial, biennial and annual- what kind of weeds do you see in your life right now? I'd like you to take a moment to define them the best way you can as either annual, biennial or perennial. Here are some thoughts to help you:

- **Annual**- it is within my capability to decide today and begin seeing immediate change in this area. *{Maybe this is an area that you've just been putting off for some time now. You know it has to change but you keep giving excuses.}*
- **Biennial**- this is an area where you've tried to change but keep finding yourself back in the same trap again. *{You know what's right, you've tried to pursue it but somehow you can't seem to gain the victory by yourself. It feels like a stronghold in your life - Get some help. Maybe a counsellor, maybe a pastor, but get some help.}*
- **Perennial**- This is an area that seems to come back often. You do well in it today but fail badly at it tomorrow. *{It's not that you're bound in it. It's just that you have good days and bad days. It's the sin nature that needs daily crucifying}*

Learning these differences helps us achieve more by doing less because we are no longer fighting blind. Our understanding helps open our eyes so that we live like Paul who said, ***"I do not fight like I am beating the air," 1 Corinthians 9:26 BSB.*** This means we don't throw aimless punches in our fight against weeds which leads to burnout. One of the ways that believers experience burnout is when we keep throwing punches that don't result in progress. Dealing with our weeds from a place of understanding that there are various kinds of weeds helps us throw punches that are effective; punches that knock out the enemy and lead us to victory in the process.

In Leviticus, the Lord commands us not to mate different animals. This is a type that teaches us many things. Among those many lessons, I believe one of them is this; our solutions must be compatible with the problems that we are trying to solve. When weeds are dealt with using strategies that aren't compatible with them, it is as if we are mating a donkey and a horse. The result is something that can't reproduce. The inability of this offspring to reproduce is teaching us a spiritual lesson. It is teaching us that when our solutions are not compatible with the weeds that we are dealing with in our lives, our efforts will not be fruitful. So, just like Paul says that he doesn't fight like someone beating the air, we must not deal with weeds like we are mating different animals. Let us take the time to patiently learn the type of weed so that we can match it to a compatible strategy. This helps us see fruit from our labour. Fruit comes not because we are sincere because even in being sincere, we can be sincerely mistaken. Fruit comes when we allow ourselves to patiently learn to match our strategies with the weeds with which we are dealing. This is the subject of our next chapter.

CHAPTER 8

———— ✳ ————

Different Strategies for Different Weeds

Don't Bring a Knife to A Gunfight!
(American Idiom)

<u>One Size Doesn't Fit All</u>

If weeds are so different from each other, then what works in dealing with one type of weed will likely not work in dealing with another. In other words, when it comes to dealing with weeds I must have more than one strategy. A 'one size fits all strategy' will never lead to one-hundred-fold fruitfulness. That is why it is important to understand like we did in the previous chapter that weeds have differences. Learning about these differences in weeds helps us see them clearly. This is a key part of winning the battle against weeds. This understanding gives us clearer sight for this fight. When we can see clearly, we are better able to throw the kind of punches that have the power to knock out our enemy. This is the secret to choosing the right strategy. If we only have one strategy for dealing with our weeds it's likely that at some point that strategy will prove to not be enough.

But you may be asking yourself how people approach their lives and weeds with a one size fits all strategy. That is a good question. From my observation this happens when we stick to methods that were successful in our past battles without evaluating if they are still being effective in the present circumstances. When we live with this mindset, we make statements like these. I'm sure you have heard some of them.

- *"We will do business a certain way because that is how our parents did it. Since it was successful for them, it will be successful for us."*
- *"We will raise our kids the way we were raised as children regardless of how they respond to it. Our parents raised us to be successful so their methods should work on our kids."*
- *"We will run our churches the same way, today, like we did when we first planted them. If it worked for us then it should work for us today."*

These three statements are examples of what we say and do if we are approaching life from a one size fits all strategy. You probably can think of more examples of how people approach their life situations with this mentality. This mentality is often seen through our actions and attitudes and not just our words. Identifying it in our lives is less about examining what we say (our vocabulary) and more about examining how we live (our attitudes and behaviour). Our behaviour and attitudes are what reveals whether or not we are plagued by this mentality. Honestly examining and evaluating how we live is what will help us see if we are bringing a knife to a gun battle as the Americans say!

On the surface, some of the above statements and behaviours may even sound noble. In reality, they are toxic. They do not lead to victory in dealing with weeds and neither do they lead to victory in life generally. This one size fits all strategy produces three negative behaviours in us.

1. **Sticking to methods without evaluating fruitfulness**. In other words, it prioritises activity over productivity.
2. **Loyalty to methods at the expense of results**. In other words, it creates a culture where we favour tradition over fruitfulness
3. **Mistaking methods and strategies for principles**. It creates an environment where we begin breeding sacred cows over an open and honest policy.

Good Strategies Produce Good Fruit

All three of the above negative mindsets result in us being unfruitful. This happens because they stop us from effectively dealing with our weeds. The first negative effect of weeds in our lives is to reduce or completely stop our fruitfulness. It is for this very purpose that we should always be open to changing our strategy when the need arises. We should be open to change when it comes to dealing with weeds because the goal is fruitfulness. Our goal is not to prove that one method is superior to another. Jesus teaches us this principle when he says, **"Wisdom is proved right by all its results."** **Luke 7:35 NOG.** James also alludes to this when he says that our wisdom (or in other words our strategies) must be measured by the quality of the results it produces. **"The wisdom that comes from heaven is ... full of mercy and good fruit." James 3:7 NIV**. If the fruit is not good, the strategy is not right. This is regardless of my attachment and loyalty to the strategy. It may even be a strategy that produced good fruit in previous seasons but if the fruit is not good right now, then the strategy needs to be reviewed. Oftentimes letting go of a strategy that once worked can be really challenging. We get attached to how we get things done and, without realising it, we end up idolising our method because it has been so effective in the past. A strategy that served us well in the past can eventually become a master over us and the organisations we lead. This is a bad place to be.

Our strategies need to serve us, they must not become our masters. The word strategy means, *"a plan that is intended to achieve a particular purpose" (Oxford Learner's Free Dictionary).* This means that if a behaviour or way of living is no longer taking us toward a particular purpose it is no longer a strategy. It has become something else entirely. At times, misunderstanding strategy gives birth to tradition. The word tradition is defined as, *"a belief, custom or way of doing something that has existed for a long time among a particular group of people" (Oxford Learner's Free Dictionary).* As you can see in these two definitions, if what I call strategy is no longer based on a goal, it has in fact become a tradition.

I learnt the difference between strategy and tradition through an experience that Zinty and I had. Early in our marriage, we were quite flexible when it came to scheduling our devotional time. We never really planned when it would happen. We just went with the flow each day, and yet we were pretty consistent in it, and we grew in our love for each other and in our love for the Lord. However, as we took on more responsibility in our jobs and eventually became pastors, we found that our devotional time kept suffering. We began to spend less and less time with God as a couple. Even though we liked the idea of just flowing into our devotional time we began to realise the need to schedule it otherwise it would become an afterthought. We tried many things but eventually landed on something that has served us well in the season of life that we are in. I have no doubt that when we move into a new season, we may also need to change our strategy for how we do our devotional times as a couple. Through this I learnt that the wisdom of how we were doing our devotional life as a couple had to be proved by its fruitfulness and not our preference. Otherwise, it would turn into tradition. And tradition, as we have seen, is not goal oriented.

Here's another example. When dealing with sexual temptation we flee, but when dealing with relational tension we stay and fight by doing good to our enemies. If we flee relational tension with our family the same way we flee sexual temptation with a partner who isn't willing to wait to have sex until we are married, our strategy will only work some of the time. If we overcome relational tension by doing good to those who despise us and it works so well that we try to overcome sexual temptation by giving in to the demands of our partner, our strategy will only work some of the time. And what is the result of all this? Some weeds in our lives will never go away and we will only be partly fruitful like the ground that produced thirty times or sixty times what was planted. The ground that will produce one hundred times what was planted is the ground that will deal with all three types of weeds. This may be the reason there are three levels of fruitfulness. The thirty-fold land had dealt with only one type of weed, the sixty-fold had dealt with two types of weeds and the hundred-fold had dealt with all three types of weeds. The important insight from this quality of weeds is that weeds are different, and it takes different strategies to overcome them all.

To keep pressing on towards our goals in life, we need to be open to changing our strategies when the need arises. This is how we should choose the strategies for dealing with our weeds. True wisdom is learning to have an appreciation of the need to change when we see a lack of fruitfulness.

True wisdom holds on to only one tradition; the tradition of changing when the need to change arises. A part of learning to walk in this wisdom comes with understanding an important aspect about the nature and dynamics of change- how change was not made equal.

Change Was Not Made Equal

The Lord is One, and He never changes. There is no debating that. Yet, in His wisdom He has given us a Bible containing sixty-six books amounting to over 31,000 verses of instruction for living. Why would He need to give us so many books and verses if He is one and He never changes? The reason is because we need different strategies for the different seasons of life. We need different strategies to deal with different weeds. However, as mentioned, what is changing is the strategy and not the principle. We must learn to differentiate between these two kinds of changes: changing the principle versus changing the strategy. As we do, we grow in our openness to changing strategies as we enter new seasons or deal with different struggles because we know that we are not changing principles. This will result in fruitfulness.

A wonderful way to think about this is to tell yourself, *"Change was not made equal."* Some change is nothing more than painting the same car a different colour of paint. It looks different, but is it really different? No, it is not! On the other hand, some change is like changing the engine of a vehicle. The car may look the same on the outside but is it still the same? Absolutely not. Changing how we manage our church so that we let go of unproductive habits is not turning our backs on the faith. It is like that car that has a different coat of paint but is still running on the same engine. However, maybe because of a fresh coat of paint, it gets noticed by more people along the road- a different group of people from those who knew the car before. This increases the car's ability to influence. There is some change that is necessary if we are to get better; this kind of change makes us better without making us different. However, there is another change that makes us different. It makes us think we are better, but because we have changed what must not be changed, we aren't better, we are a completely different species. That is not the change I'm discussing here.

The key in trying to learn the difference is to look at the fruit. If our attendance is dropping and our goal (fruit) is to reach more people, we may need to ask ourselves, "Is it time to give our car a fresh coat of paint?" "What changes can we make that will help us become more fruitful without us compromising our message? "As an example, we will never think about changing the fact that we preach based on the truth of the Bible, but we may consider changing how long the message is. We can consider whether it is time to offer our services online. We may consider whether it is time to modernise the way that we deliver the message so that we reach those that we haven't yet reached. So, in one sense we are changing things but, in another sense, we really aren't changing anything. This is what it means to change strategies. It is the kind of change that makes us more fruitful without compromising who we are and what we believe in. This is possible not only for churches as I have illustrated here, but it can be applied to businesses, to non-profits and most of all, this applies in our lives personally. There truly is some change that makes us better without making us different. The key to understanding and implementing this change lies in being clear on the difference between the goal and the strategy that we are using to achieve it.

We often think that there are some people who are naturally more open to change than others. I think it's possible that there is some truth to that, but the bigger reality in my observation is that the key to embracing change is not in being genetically wired to embrace it. Rather, it lies in understanding that not all change was made equal. Otherwise, the rest of us with the wrong genetics are just born to be victims and have been dealt an unfair hand by the Creator. My knowledge of the Creator is that He is good. He didn't create us to be victims, He created us to be victorious. So, this makes me conclude that openness to change is not a personality type. Everybody can grow in their openness to change. This happens when we learn to distinguish between the times when we are repainting the car and the times when we are now messing with the engine.

Our openness to change can increase because we are all wired to desire more fruitfulness (as gardens of the Lord) and when we learn that change is a part of making that happen, change is no longer a threat, it becomes our tool. So, our struggle is not with change, it is with understanding whether this is good change. Our struggle is with understanding the difference between principles and methods. And those more open to change are those who learn to understand, "change was not made equal."

Evaluating By the Fruit

Everything in our lives that is judged by its fruit has been judged well. The reason for this is simple. We were created to be fruitful, and fruit is what we should hope to see when we look at our lives. We are gardens, planted by the Lord, for his glory. We were created to be fruitful. So, if we are being unfruitful in some area of our lives, we must be open to changing our strategies for managing it. If our marriages are not producing the fruit of a holy life, we must be open to changing some of the practices that we inherited from our parents. If our careers have plateaued and we do not feel that we are fulfilling our destiny we must be open to change so that we can get back on the course marked out for us by our Father in heaven before the foundations of the world were laid.

We must open our minds to the possibility that to get better we need to embrace a different strategy because weeds are different. And at various stages of our lives, we encounter a new kind of weed that requires that we apply different methods to those we used in the past. This is what the Bible means when it teaches us that, **"Don't become so well-adjusted to your culture that you fit into it without even thinking. Instead, fix your attention on God. You'll be changed from the inside out. Readily recognize what he wants from you, and quickly respond to it. Unlike the culture around you, always dragging you down to its level of immaturity, God brings the best out of you, develops well-formed maturity in you." Romans 12:2 MSG**

So, how then do we apply the understanding of this quality of weeds? By developing a mindset that evaluates our lives, our organisations, our relationships on their fruitfulness not tradition, fruitfulness not religion, fruitfulness not status, fruitfulness not … anything else. Anything in our lives that is not evaluated on fruitfulness quickly becomes a hiding place for weeds. This is because weeds attack our fruitfulness before anything else. Therefore, judging our lives by fruitfulness is one of the safest ways of guarding against weeds. And the fruitfulness that every believer needs to be producing, the fruitfulness that glorifies God is the fruit of the Spirit first before it is the fruit of all the ministry that we do for Him.

If we don't measure that fruitfulness honestly, it is possible to have weeds but still not detect them. We need to evaluate fruitfulness because eventually, if we do not, our soul is the one that is at risk as we saw in chapter one. Jesus when teaching about fruitfulness said that **"He *(The Father)* cuts off every branch in me that bears no fruit." John 15:2 NIV** (emphasis added by author). Initially, when I read this verse, it seemed harsh to me. But having learned about how fruitfulness works I realised something. I realised that for a branch to be considered unfruitful it means that it has been given many years of opportunities to be fruitful and it is only after many chances that the Father eventually cuts off a branch. A branch is not considered unfruitful after one season of growth. No. We have several chances to deal with weeds. Let's take them. Because weeds aren't just after our fruitfulness, they are after our soul. So, we ought to deal with them before they deal with us.

Be Careful of the Green

In the Gospel of Mark, Jesus teaches us an important lesson about measuring fruitfulness. *"When he came to it (the fig tree), he found nothing but leaves, for it was not the season for figs. 14 And he said to it, "May no one ever eat fruit from you again," Mark 11:13-14 ESV* This tree was green and looked good from afar, but when Jesus drew closer, there was no fruit. Even a garden with weeds can look beautiful and, sometimes, even fruitful from afar. This is because from afar all that we see is green. But the real test comes when we come closer and look deeper just like Jesus did when He came to the fig tree. As we measure fruitfulness, we need to be careful to not be deceived by the areas in our life that are green because **weeds are also green.**

Weeds being green speaks of their deceptive nature. We often look at plants from afar and assume that because they are green, they must be productive. However, productivity is not measured by the colour of the tree. Productivity is measured by fruit. In saying weeds are green I am saying that we must not allow ourselves to be fooled by how certain things look from afar. We must take a closer look to see if they are truly being productive. Weeds are green just like our plants, but they don't produce the required fruit. If a plant is green, it confirms to you and me that it is taking nutrients from us. Green confirms that we have invested in it somehow and therefore it is expected to produce fruit. So, when I inspect it and don't find fruit, I must consider it a threat because it has been taking from my soil (my heart), but it is not giving back.

In our lives, green represents things that are active but not productive; things that cause us to be on the move without that movement resulting in progress. Examples of these things in our lives include- meetings that all staff members are required to attend even though what's being discussed in the meeting is of minimal relevance to some of the staff present; habits that have become second nature but do not grow me in the area of my calling; and projects that we are engaged in (maybe some that we even inherited from the previous leadership) but do not add to the vision of the organization in a significant way. We ought to stop and take a closer look at each of these kinds of green plants in our lives to see if they are more than just green, but also fruitful. If they do not have fruit, by definition they are weeds and must be cut down. This matters because ***when we don't cut down the excess green, we are unintentionally stunting productivity from the green that is producing fruit.*** Weeds take away our margin. If we find ourselves constantly dealing with a full schedule, we ought to stop and ask God to show us what weeds we need to uproot from our garden. Some weeds may even be potential plants and flowers in another garden but because they originate from a foreign seed, they are weeds in my garden. The only plants that must grow in our gardens are the ones that originate from the seed of God's Word; His Rhema quickened word that speaks of His specific purpose for me.

So, the question is, "what fig trees do we have in our lives that look good from afar but every time we move closer to try and enjoy some fruit, we are disappointed?" Remember that even a garden with weeds can look beautiful and, sometimes, even fruitful from afar. This is because from afar all that we see is green. Let's be intentional to test true fruitfulness by coming closer and looking deeper just like Jesus did when He came to the fig tree.

Reflection

Question: Based on the fruit (or lack of it), in what area of my life do I need to embrace the need to change my strategy so that I begin to be fruitful, or I become more fruitful?

Answer:

_____

_____

_____

_____

_____

Question: Why have I been reluctant to change my strategies?

Answer:

_____

_____

_____

_____

_____

Question: In this area, what are the things that I need to be open to changing (like the colour of the car) and what are the things that must never be touched (the principles, like the engine of the car)?

Answer:

_____

_____

_____

_____

_____

Question: In embracing change, what new strategies could I try in order to become more fruitful in this area?

Answer:

_____

_____

_____

_____

_____

Quality 3

✳

Weeds Thrive in Fertile Soil

CHAPTER 9

✳

Where Weeds Grow,
Seeds can also Grow

"...the crops grew ..., but also weeds"
Matthew 13:26 Voice Translation

<u>Revelation</u>

We had a small portion of land in front of our living room where we chose to plant some flowers. After initially seeming to grow and blossom, all the flowers planted on this portion of land wilted and died. Due to our humble gardening skills and the fact that we were very new to this, we didn't understand why these flowers had behaved the way they did. So, we decided to plant again and give this project a second chance (after all, our God is a God of second chances, right? :-)). We planted on this portion of land for a second time, and, to our frustration, the same thing happened. We persisted and tried planting something different in this same space but, lo and behold, the result was remarkably similar, almost identical, in fact. It was then that I took some time to observe this portion of land. While observing it, I compared it to the other portions of land that were doing quite well relative to this one. As I made the comparison of these different portions of land, one thing immediately stood out to me. I realised that, unlike the others, this part of the garden had no weeds growing in it. I

85

thought about what the reason for this could have been for a few moments. Then it hit me! A light bulb went on and I realised that the issue wasn't the seed (or our humble gardening techniques. Phew! :-)). Rather, the issue was with the soil. I can still feel and remember my excitement as I shared my observation with Zinty.

Over this process of time and some trial and error, Zinty and I had learnt an especially important spiritual lesson from our garden. The lesson, the revelation, was this: weeds grow and flourish where seeds can also grow and flourish. This means that when we have weeds in our churches, businesses, or personal lives that we need to deal with-as frustrating as that can be- it is also a good sign. It is a sign that our churches, businesses, and lives have the capacity for fruitfulness. While it is true that weeds most definitely mean we have some work to do, this should also be an encouragement to us because if we are having to deal with weeds, we have the raw materials for a fruitful life. Weeds can be a source of great discouragement, but it doesn't have to be that way. Think about it this way- no-one has ever had to deal with a weed problem in the desert. So, if you have weeds, thank God you're not a desert! Yes, you have some work to do, but isn't it better to have work to do than to be a spiritual desert?

Friend Of Sinners

Weeds, by their very nature, confirm the potential of our gardens to be fruitful. Therefore, when we see in ourselves or come across people that are producing a lot of bad fruit in their lives, we must not despair. Rather, we must see through the forest of weeds into the God given potential that they have to be fruitful. This may be the reason Jesus was known as a friend of sinners.

Jesus did not allow weeds in people's lives to intimidate him and cause him to shy away from them. He allowed himself to see through the sin. And, I believe, that is part of the reason He was able to become friends with many of them. In life, sometimes the people who have gone on to be fruitful in the kingdom of God, are the ones who started off as big sinners causing chaos and heartache for their parents, leaders, and the society at large. The Apostle Paul is an example of this. He was known for persecuting the Church and even gave his approval when Stephen, the first martyr of the New Testament Church, was killed. However, after his conversion, Paul went on to have a fruitful ministry as a missionary. He spearheaded the movement to bring the Gospel to the Gentiles (people who are not born Jewish). We can see that from this great sinner with undoubtedly many weeds in his life came a missionary and an apostle who lived a very fruitful life, a life that glorified God. He went from being a garden with many weeds to being a garden with much fruit. His life experienced a great turnaround. And this turnaround shouldn't be as surprising when you look at the observation about weeds that we are discussing in this chapter. The weeds flourishing in his life showed the capability that he had to be a very fruitful garden since, "weeds flourish where seed can flourish too."

Paul, when instructing his son in the faith, Timothy, about Jesus declares that *"Christ came to save sinners." 1 Timothy 1:15a NKJV* I found this to be very profound. Christ didn't come for those who think they are righteous. He came for those who realise they have a sin problem. He came to save sinners. What is even more profound is the statement Paul made following his declaration of Christ coming to save sinners. He said, *"of which I am chief." 1 Timothy 1:15b NKJV.* What Paul is saying here is that he is a prime example of Christ's power to perform this great turnaround in any human being. He is declaring that, in the lives of those that the world looks at and sees nothing but weeds, it is possible for there to be a great and miraculous turnaround because Christ came. "Christ came to save sinners" means Jesus came for the kinds of people that the world has given up on- the ones that the world sees as lost causes. He came not just to befriend them; He came in the hope that He would be used by the Father to save them.

THE ENEMY DOESN'T FIGHT FAIR

As we make this observation, there is another important question that we ought to try and answer. The question of, "Why?" Why do we see this trend repeated so often in the lives of those who go on to make a significant impact in the kingdom of God.?" "Why is it that, oftentimes, those who go on to greater fruitfulness seem to need lengthy preparations where the Lord helps them deal with and overcome many weeds?" Having taken some time to think about it, I concluded that it is because the enemy doesn't fight fair. Let me illustrate this truth using the account of the miraculous healing of a demon possessed man by Jesus.

When healing the demon possessed man, Jesus asked the demon a simple question, ""**What is your name?**" In his response to Jesus' question, we learn about this very sinister tactic of the enemy of our souls. The demon replied, **"My name is Legion, because there are many of us inside this man." (Mark 5:9 NLT).** Now, as I listened to this answer, I began asking myself the question, why would many demons gang up on one person? Surely one demon should be enough! But somehow this man had a legion of them residing in him. One of the reasons the enemy does this, is the same as the reason people gang up on an opponent when a fight breaks out. People gang up on an opponent because they know that they are weaker than their opponent and so, in order to win the fight, they choose to fight unfairly by forming a gang.

The enemy needs to use this unfair tactic in order to give himself an advantage (he doesn't play fair, so he doesn't mind gaining an advantage through unjust means). Because of this, the result, as we see in this case, is that there were many demons against one man. This is the reason, in the spirit as it is in nature, fertile gardens often have many weeds. It is because the enemy of our souls, knowing his weakness, chooses to fight unfairly in the hope that he can give himself an advantage. Often, he will try and gang up on a person early, planting many weeds in their life in the hope that he can defeat them before what they possess ever comes to the light. This is the reason this man had a legion of demons in him. This is also the reason Mary Magdalene was in a similar situation- she needed Jesus to cast out seven demons from her! (Luke 8:2). Throughout the Bible we see that the enemy has this tendency of not fighting fairly in his battle against the children of the light.

If we continue to observe the progression of the life of this man who was freed from a legion of demons, we will see something remarkably interesting. When he began obeying Jesus and fulfilling his purpose, the fruit of his life was so much that it resulted in ten cities receiving the Good News about Jesus Christ. This man, therefore, had been destined to be a giant in the faith doing wonderful things for the kingdom of God and it seems to me that this is the reason the Devil tried to gang up on him using a legion of demons to keep him down. We can conclude that this man dealt with many demons not because he was weak and insignificant, but because he was a potential giant and the enemy, using dirty tactics, was fighting to try and keep a good man down. This is what I mean when I say that the enemy doesn't fight fair.

What Does This Mean for You?

Let's turn our attention to what this means for us. Firstly, **I would like you to know that the enemy still uses this same tactic today.** If, as you've been living your life, you have felt attacked from many directions, understand that it is not because you're weak and insignificant. It is not because you possess the wrong genes or because you come from the wrong side of town. No! It is because you possess within you the ability to cause real damage to the kingdom of darkness and the enemy is resorting to dirty tactics to stop you. Do not despair. Do not give up. Do not turn back. Trust in God's ability to set you free like He did with the man oppressed by a legion of demons. You are destined to be more than what you see right now. You are destined to be more than what your current circumstances and upbringing seem to say about you right now. The key to fulfilling your purpose is to learn to decode the reason for the enemy's attack upon your life differently when it comes to dealing with weeds. You've been ganged up on, *"because the Spirit who lives in you is greater than the spirit who lives in the world." 1 John 4:4b NLT* **You are not fighting this battle because you are weak.** You are fighting this battle because you have the potential to be a giant in the faith. The enemy, knowing you are a potential giant that can destroy his kingdom, keeps devising ways to stop you from bringing out this treasure that God has placed in you. But, because you have the Holy Spirit in you, always remember that you are a powerful person. You are so powerful in fact that the world often misunderstands you, underestimates you and, consequently, tries to limit you. Being Spirit-filled and Spirit-led has always been accompanied with being underestimated by this world. This is what Jesus meant when He said, *"The wind blows wherever it wishes; you hear the sound it makes, but you do not know where it comes from or where it is going. It is like that with everyone who is born of the Spirit." John 3:8 GNT.* This is a very carefully chosen analogy by Jesus because wind is the cleanest source of energy in the world. It was intentionally chosen by Jesus to teach us that as we walk according to the Spirit, we can be like wind that produces no negative impact on the environment when generating energy. It is completely clean. A Spirit-filled person is an immensely powerful person, but they must be careful of the trap of weeds that the enemy tries to plant in their lives. Sowing weeds in our lives is the enemy's way of trying to pervert and pollute the wind of God that is blowing through us.

Secondly, understanding this quality of weeds also means that we must begin to view others differently. This will be the subject of our next chapter, Visualisation. But before concluding this chapter I would like to give you a small caution.

A Caution for Believers

Learning that the enemy doesn't fight fair against God's people is also a caution for us as believers. We must be careful to not gang up on others because when people gang up against someone, oftentimes it is not the Holy Spirit motivating that work. Often, the enemy deceives the simple and the offended into ganging up against God's servants and the work that He has called them to accomplish. Let us be careful of being a part of majorities that are not founded on and motivated by truth. Let us be careful whom we touch when we are in the majority because without intending, we can find that we have touched and wounded the Lord's anointed one. We must be careful about our associations because without realising it they affect how we think towards God's people. *David Schwartz once said, "How we think is directly affected by the group we're in. Be sure you're in the flock that thinks right."* We must be careful which gang, which crew, which flock we are in because the Lord will hold us accountable if we come against His servants. The Holy Spirit is gentle and kind. He does not inspire us to attack people when they are down or have erred in some way. We see this often in our day when people boycott buying a product because of one unsubstantiated rumour about the CEO of that company. By the time the truth is revealed a person's life and reputation has long been ruined. To protect ourselves from the deception that causes us to be in the majority that gangs up on the righteous, James 1:19 & 20 NLT has some valuable advice that we would do well to apply. *"You must be quick to listen, slow to speak and slow to get angry. Human anger does not produce the righteousness God desires."* When we apply this wisdom, we will be less likely to find ourselves in groups of people that are motivated by unrighteous anger and are ganging up against the innocent. Let us use this wisdom from James to challenge the movements that we are a part of, the groups that we associate ourselves with, and the people that we are outspoken against on social media. Let us allow this wisdom to help us stop and evaluate whether our gang, our crew, our tribe is still motivated by a righteous cause. This is the key to being in the majority. Let's realize that the majority is not where there are more people, the majority is where the Lord is. The majority is always on the side of truth motivated by love and expressed through mercy. Truth without love leads to harsh judgements. Love without truth gives licence to sin and unrighteousness. Truth motivated by love expresses itself in mercy and that is the side that God is on. The side that Jesus is on is where the majority is, regardless of how many people choose that side. That is why we need to learn and grow in visualisation. Let us explore this together in the next chapter.

Chapter 10

❋

Visualisation

*'Buy also some ointment to put on your eyes,
so that you may see.'*
Revelation 3:18 GNT

Parents who look at their children based only on the children's current behaviour are opening themselves up to many opportunities for discouragement. This is because children go through many stages of development. At each stage, the children develop behaviours and tendencies that can frustrate almost any parent. However, if you take time to observe parents you will realise that not all parents are frustrated by this. Some seem to be able to still love, care for and see the best in their children regardless of the frustrations that may be on offer. How do they do this? Well, one of the reasons that they are able to do this is because they see and visualise their children not just as they are today but as what they can be in the future. They visualise the potential father who needs to be taught how to lead himself so he can eventually lead his own home. They visualise the potential CEO who needs a good education so he can learn to manage his or her company successfully. They visualise the potential mother who needs to be taught to be patient so she can be patient with her own children one day.

When we grow in the understanding that weeds grow where the ground has potential to be fruitful, our view of people is positively affected. This understanding is like ointment to our eyes; it helps us see and love people just like Jesus sees and loves them. It helps us overcome the prejudice of looking at people as lost causes. It saves us from the very toxic thinking that, 'some people have been damaged beyond repair." When we see people, even while they are sinning, we must train ourselves to see beyond their sin. When we allow ourselves to see things this way, we position ourselves to participate in God's effort to set them free. In the same way that God used Jesus to set a man free from a legion of demons and God used Ananias to guide Paul into his destiny, God is looking for someone that he can trust to launch the 'Paul' of our generation into his destiny. And you could be that person! The key is to have an openness of heart and mind to see sinners as potential winners.

Obviously, this is a challenge. It is a challenge to our natural way of viewing and dealing with people. It is also a challenge for us not to shun those that the world has labelled as sinners [though, in reality, we know that all have sinned and need a Saviour]. It is a challenge for us to train ourselves to look at the so-called sinners so differently that we can befriend them long enough to not just become their friends but, God-willing, to also influence them to salvation. We are being challenged to see Paul the apostle while we're still looking at Saul the persecutor; to see Gideon the mighty man of valour while still staring at Gideon the coward hiding from conflict.

Mark Schwartz, in his book "The Magic of Thinking Big," speaks about this way of seeing people as visualisation. He says that one of the keys to successful living is to, ***"Look at things not as they are but as they can be. Visualisation adds value to everything."*** God wants to wash our eyes and give us the kind of sight that allows us to see people not as they are but as what they could be when His grace washes over them. Though challenging, there is a great benefit to growing in this way of viewing people. As I pondered Paul's words ***(that Christ came to save sinners)*** and Mark Schwartz's version of them, I realised that this literally applies to everything in life.

We see from the above example of parenting that visualizing what our children can be, not just what they are now, helps us to manage well and deal wisely with the less-than-ideal tendencies that they develop as they mature. Instead of just being frustrated, we begin to see these tendencies as opportunities to gain a greater understanding of their capabilities and how we can help them fulfil their potential. Sometimes there's mischief that needs addressing and disciplining that needs to be done. However, oftentimes, visualising what our children can be and not just what they are right now, helps us appreciate them and celebrate their uniqueness instead of being frustrated by their immaturity. Children are just one of the many examples where this thinking can help us become more fruitful. This can also be applied to how we deal with our employees or how we manage our volunteer teams in charitable organisations. In fact, like Dr Schwartz said, *"Visualisation adds value to everything."* So, pause and take a moment to reflect by answering this question, "Is there a person or an area of your life that can benefit from you applying the principle of visualisation; seeing people/things not as they are but as they can be?" If your life resembles mine in any way, I'm sure there's more than just one area. Let's continue.

Once, when my father was teaching me about leadership, he told me that, *"if there is no good for people to do, then it's likely that they will be up to no good."* Through this lesson, he taught me to manage people differently when I find them up to no good. He taught me to give people a chance to change by giving them an opportunity to do good instead of quickly punishing them because I found them up to no good. As a leader this has helped me greatly. I am constantly positively surprised by how people's lives turn around when they are given an opportunity to do good. It is almost like they transform and become a new person sometimes. All because they were visualised differently and given an opportunity to do good in place of being up to no good. I have never forgotten this lesson and I share it with you today, assuring you that there are some around you who, given a chance, will turn from the path of 'up to no good' onto the highway of 'doing good.' And you can be the one to give them that chance. Through visualisation you learn to separate what is major from what is minor. You learn to show grace and let go of what is minor while using wisdom to correctly manage what is major. This all grows out of understanding that weeds can be a sign of a person's potential to be fruitful.

But how is visualisation developed? How can you as a parent, as a friend, as an employer, as a leader or as a pastor, develop your ability to walk in the art and wisdom of visualisation? To develop your ability to positively visualise people you must understand two universal truths about humanity:

1. PEOPLE ARE OFTEN A MIXTURE.
2. MERCY MAKES PEOPLE BETTER.

We will spend the rest of this chapter discussing these two keys to becoming a master at positively visualising people.

1. People Are Often a Mixture

Because of the fallen nature that we are dealing with on this side of eternity, people are rarely 100% of one thing. More often than not there is a mixture of seeds and weeds growing in each of us. Jesus gives us a glimpse of this tendency in humans in his parable of the wheat and the weeds when He said, **"When the crop began to grow and produce grain, the weeds also grew." Matthew 13:26 NLT.** This parable teaches us that inside most of us there is a mixture of seeds and weeds growing. The seeds produce the good that we see, and the weeds produce the bad. The seeds produce the sweet and pleasant side of our humanity, kind of like Side A of a cassette tape. The weeds produce side B- the thorny, bitter, and ultimately unfruitful side of us and others. If we are to appreciate people for who they are, instead of shaming them for who they are not, it is important to realise and understand that they, just like us, are a work in progress. They have some seeds growing for which they must be encouraged and commended. And they also have some weeds growing for which they need to be gently challenged and corrected.

As we understand this universal truth about humanity our eyes are opened to the opportunity to put into practice the power of visualisation. We do this by training ourselves to see, meditate on and celebrate their side A qualities while realising and accepting that this same person still has a journey to walk in dealing with the side B of their character. The alternative, which I do not recommend, is to classify someone as a completely bad person because we had an unpleasant side B experience with them. When we do this, we are failing to appreciate that though we had an unpleasant experience with them that points to weeds, it does not negate the fact that there are some exceptionally good things about that person too that deserve to be celebrated. Here are a couple of symptoms of this kind of thinking:

- a constant **breakdown of relationships**
- a tendency to be involved in **many misunderstandings** often over trivial things.
- a tendency to have **cliques rather than true communities**. This is when we have friends of only one socio-economic status, race, or political persuasion. Most of the time these friends are of the same socio-economic status, race, political persuasion, church background, etc as we are.
- **difficulty in forgiving** offences and taking steps towards reconciling with those who offend us and making it hard for people to apologise to us.

All these symptoms stem from focusing on the weeds (or side B) of a person so much that we forget that in almost every human being on the planet there is a mixture of both side A and side B.

The better way to deal with people, which I highly recommend, is to love people with unconditional love. We do this by embracing this universal truth that there is often a mixture in others as well as in ourselves. When we embrace this understanding and thinking towards others our lives will be marked by three distinct qualities that help us succeed in making friends with sinners like Jesus did:

1. We will be quick to give others the **benefit of the doubt** when misunderstandings arise. This will help us grow in our willingness and ability to **forgive and release offences**, not just the small ones but the bigger ones too.
2. We will grow in our ability and willingness to take steps towards reconciliation when relationships have been broken. Often, we'll find that we are able to take the first step to mend things in a fractured relationship.
3. Our friendship circles will grow and become diverse in terms of race, political persuasion, socio economic status among other qualities. This happens as a result of the openness of heart that understanding the mixture in people brings. It helps us to hear and make room, in our hearts and lives, for people from a different

life viewpoint. In summary, we build a true community around ourselves, helping many people feel a genuine sense of belonging.

2. Mercy Makes People Better

Because of the mixture that exists in most people, it is easy to look at those around us and quickly see faults in them for which we can justifiably criticize them. In fact, after a while, we can get to the point where we can predict when those closest to us will fail to keep their promises, omit to put down the toilet seat after using it or even forget to add salt to the food when they cook. However, this criticism does not make them better (neither does it make you better, in fact a critical spirit causes the one who is critical to become bitter, not better). Criticism leaves people worse, not better. Mercy on the other hand is different. It has the effect of making people better when it is generously applied in place of criticism. To become good at visualisation you will need to understand how to replace criticism and judgment with mercy because "mercy makes people better,". Criticism, judgement and fault finding doesn't. This is the second universal truth about humanity that when applied to those around us- at home, work, church, on the highway and the pavement- causes us to become better at visualisation.

Even after negative experiences with a person, we need to somehow be able to still find and focus on the good in that person. We need to have the capability to forget wrongs, maybe not in an intellectual way but definitely in our emotions and mindset about that person. It is impossible to continuously replay offences in our minds and still be good at visualization.

Jesus is the best example of this ability to show mercy instead of giving criticism and judgement. Leading up to His crucifixion, Peter (who was one of the three inner circle disciples) denied him three times! This must have hurt, and yet after He rose from the dead, Jesus didn't criticize and condemn Peter. Instead, He commissioned him to be a pillar in His church by taking care of those who were about to come to salvation. How come Jesus didn't give Peter a tough time? How come He didn't give him a tongue lashing in front of the other disciples? What did He know that gave him the confidence to immediately reinstate Peter the way He did? I think it's because he saw the mixture in Peter's heart (how in one moment Peter declared a revelation that would become the foundation on which Jesus would build the New Testament church and in the very next moment the enemy spoke through him to try and tempt Jesus into not going to the cross). In seeing and understanding this mixture, Jesus chose mercy over criticism and judgement. He chose this because He understood and applied this second universal truth about people that 'mercy makes people better.'

In Matthew 9, we see an encounter between Jesus and the Pharisees that gives us another glimpse into the power of mercy. The Pharisees were trying to make people better by upholding the law to the point that they made the law an idol. They were overly critical and judgemental in their approach to others and even toward Jesus who was having dinner with many tax collectors and sinners. Jesus, in an effort to try and help them grow in visualisation, responded by encouraging them to go and learn why God loves mercy saying, ***"Go and learn what this means: 'I desire mercy, not sacrifice.' For I have not come to call the righteous, but sinners." Matthew 9:13 NIV.*** As I took some time to observe and learn like Jesus told them to do, I realised that one of the reasons God loves mercy is because mercy makes people better. Think about this question for a moment and try to answer it after taking a moment to reflect on your life. ***"Around which people do you thrive? Is it around people who criticise every single mistake you make and point out your flaws or is it around people who see the best in you even when you sometimes don't live up to it?"*** I'm sure it is the latter.

Mercy is so powerful that God has chosen to view us and act towards us motivated by mercy and kindness. Paul expressed it this way, ***"Don't you see how wonderfully kind, tolerant, and patient God is with you? Does this mean nothing to you? Can't you see that his kindness is intended to turn you from your sin? "Romans 2:4 NLT.***

Jesus wants us all, not just the Pharisees, to learn, understand and show mercy because it is mercy, not our judgemental attitudes that help people overcome their weeds and live a fruitful life. Jesus is still encouraging His followers today to learn and understand His desire for mercy over judgement. When we take time to learn mercy, I believe that we will come to the same conclusion that I came to- mercy makes people better. God's mercy builds us up instead of tearing us down because of the mistakes that we have made in the past. Similarly, our mercy is used by God to build people up instead of tearing them down by using their past mistakes against them.

Understanding mercy empowers us to practice the principle of visualisation and this saves us from the Pharisee mentality. However, if we do not understand mercy- if we do not understand that those with weeds have potential to be fruitful- we are in danger of coming under the same deception that the Pharisees had. This is a deception that blinds us to our faults and makes us think that we are superior. It's a deception so strong that it caused them to fail to recognise the Messiah- the One sent to save them from their weeds- even when He was standing right in front of them. This deception ultimately caused them to participate in His crucifixion.

There is an important lesson to learn from the Pharisees here. If we don't understand mercy, we may end up crucifying the very people that the Lord wants to use to save us and our generation from weeds. God is powerful enough that even our crucifixion of His servant won't thwart His plan but rather will help fulfil it. However, there is a great judgement that comes upon those who do the crucifying. Do not be that person! Let me encourage you to be the one who shows mercy. Whenever you're dealing with people, err on the side of mercy. Favour the most merciful course of action. Give the benefit of the doubt. Choose to see people not as they are today but as they can be in future because even in a man possessed by a legion of demons there is potential of an evangelist that God has chosen to deliver ten cities. (Mark 5:1-20). Thankfully, if you find that you aren't as merciful as you would like to be, or if you feel that God is calling you to express His mercy to others in a deeper way, this is something that you can develop. Let's talk briefly about how to develop it in your life.

Mercy is developed through these three choices.

1. **Remembering that God showed me mercy.** The book of Titus teaches us that when we remember that *"He (God) saved us, not because of righteous things we had done, but because of his mercy." Titus 3:5aNIV*, it results in us doing good, *"insist on these teachings so that all who trust in God will devote themselves to doing good." Titus 3:8 NLT.* I believe one of the

good acts that results from this remembrance is showing the same mercy that we received from God. So, if mercy has become a little difficult to show, the problem is not the people we are dealing with, our personality types or the way things are these days. No. The problem may simply be that we have forgotten the mercy that we received. And, according to the book of Titus, if we spend time remembering the mercy we received, one of the results of that remembrance is that we will devote ourselves to the good act of showing mercy to others.

2. **Responding Right to injustices and hardships.** Mercy is developed in us when we respond with meekness and humility when faced with unfair situations. When we do this, we are making room for the Lord to rescue us by the power of His mercy. This dependence on God softens our hearts and builds the same nature of being merciful to others in us. However, if we choose to respond to hardship by hardening our hearts and blaming everyone around us including God, we miss the opportunity for mercy to be built in us. The result is that we will not have the nature of God to show mercy to others in their moments of need because it was never built in us when we went through our moments of need. When faced with unfairness and injustices always remember that "the humble response is always the wise response. "The Lord will fight the battles of those who leave the fighting to Him; *"The battle depends on God, not on you." 2 Chronicles 20:15b GNT*

3. **Releasing-** Mercy, finally is learned through the practice of actually showing mercy to people. If this mercy topic is still not making sense to you, just try being merciful to someone and then watch what it does to them (and to you). Watch how your husband responds to you when he fails to keep a promise that he made to you and instead of shoving that failure in his face and shaming him, you simply excuse the mistake that he made and instead respond with a loving action towards him. Watch how your employees respond when they receive an unexpected bonus at the end of the month even though their work deserved a reprimand and maybe even a dismissal (this is not about rewarding bad behaviour, but about allowing God to help you show kindness

to those who need it even when they just let you down.) Releasing mercy becomes easier when we apply the technique of asking ourselves, "What if it was me?" Mercy becomes obvious when we put ourselves in the situation of the person that we are dealing with because we all need mercy and we all desire for it to be shown to us in our time of need. By choosing to show mercy we are choosing to love people well.

Conclusion

As we choose this way of living, here is a final encouragement: we are not alone. Jesus Christ is not only our example of this, but He is also our Shepherd as we live it out. He can guide us on this journey of learning how to visualise people, businesses, communities, churches, and anything in our world. Seeing not as it is now but as it can be on the other side of His mercy. If we invite Him on our journey, Jesus is willing and able to give us new eyes so that we can see people the way that He does. The key in all this is to approach all of our life with a pure heart that is surrendered to Jesus. The Bible teaches us that *"Everything is pure to those whose hearts are pure. But nothing is pure to those who are corrupt and unbelieving, because their minds and consciences are corrupted." Titus 1: 15 NLT.* Purifying our motives positions us to see ourselves the way God sees us. It also helps us see others the way God sees them. God, who sees the end from the beginning, sees Paul while everyone else is still seeing Saul. God sees people as they can be not just as they are today and through purifying our hearts, intentions, and motives, we too are given the blessing of being able to see people as He does- to see them as they can be, not just as they are today.

Are there any people in your sphere of influence who are literally going the opposite direction to God's instruction? Persevere with them, pray for them, perhaps they are the ones who will one day usher in a revival that saves your city, your company, or your church. Perhaps they are the Nicky Cruz of our day who went from being a gangster to an evangelist who has ministered to nearly fifty million people in person and has authored seventeen books. Perhaps they are the Dawson Trotmans of our day. Dawson Trotman went from being a onetime juvenile delinquent, who was also guilty of stealing, to being a youth-evangelist who founded Navigators. Navigators is now an international, interdenominational Christian ministry whose vision is to know Christ, make Him known, and help others do the same.

Dawson Trotman, who lost his life while trying to rescue a girl from drowning experienced such a turnaround and was so committed to serving others that even in his death he died serving and trying to save others. One of the famous statements that he made expresses well what it means to believe in the God of great turnarounds. He said, *"Soul winners are not soul winners because of what they know, but because of Who they know, and how well they know Him, and how much they long for others to know Him."* As we know and understand God and the mercy that He gives, we will see many turnarounds in our cities, organisations, churches, families and even in ourselves. This will happen as we grow in learning to add value to people by visualizing people not as they are but as they could be when His grace washes over them. Amen!

Reflection.

- Which areas of my life am I frustrated with most often? How could this frustration be pointing me towards possible fertile ground in that area?

_____

_____

_____

_____

_____

- In this same area, what are the weeds that I need to get rid of and what are the seeds that I need to nurture to maturity and fruitfulness?

  _____

  _____

  _____

  _____

  _____

- In dealing with weeds in my life, what one thing can I do based on what I have learned today to help me increase my fruitfulness as a garden of the Lord?

  _____

  _____

  _____

  _____

  _____

A Final Thought on Dealing with Weeds

CHAPTER 11

✳

Keep Your Heart Watered

"In the last days,' God says, 'I will pour out my Spirit upon all people." - Acts 2:17 NLT

'The living water of God's Word nourishes and nurtures my heart's garden' (Sarah Geringer)

Journey In Keeping My Heart Well-Watered

When I started off as a volunteer and eventually a staff member in our church, I was full of eagerness and zeal. I was in love with the Lord and in love with His church and it was this love that fuelled my service. I had a well-watered garden. This was the case because, from early on in my salvation experience, I had been taught the importance of diligently reading my Bible and praying daily. I decided to put this teaching into practice. I frequently spent time in personal prayer and reading the Bible. So, even though I couldn't have expressed it this way back then, I look back now, and I realise that I came into full-time ministry with a well-watered garden. This made me a very joyful person who served with zeal and eagerness.

But that zeal and eagerness was gradually punctured as I experienced disappointments and picked up offences along the way. This came with an increase in busyness as my wife and I took on more responsibility in the ministry. Despite all this we continued to serve as we'd always done. However, because of all these weights that I was now carrying in my soul, I slowly began to neglect prayer and reading the Bible. These practices that had been foundational at the beginning were now dying a slow and natural death. This continued for some years until things eventually came to a head and my wife and I decided to step away from staff responsibility at our church. We stepped away due to disagreements and disappointments at work, but as I look back now, I realise that the Lord had other ideas in mind. He allowed this to happen because He had a plan to lead us into a personal revival.

On the very first Sunday after we left the church we had been a part of we didn't attend a church service anywhere. We were broken, disappointed, and honestly a little relieved after having finally resolved a situation that had become uncomfortable and difficult for some time. In addition to the emotions that come naturally when dealing with the heartbreak of experiencing necessary endings, there was another feeling. This feeling couldn't be blamed on what was taking place right now. It felt more like a revelation of the state of my heart now that I didn't have the busyness of ministry responsibility to hide behind. It was a feeling of being far from God and unfamiliar with how to relate to Him personally. It was the feeling of a dry heart. We had been neglecting to water our hearts so much while focusing on serving others that we had eventually hit rock bottom.

In my time of reflection, I realised that this feeling was revealing something that I needed to take responsibility for. I couldn't blame my previous work environment, the work arrangement or the disappointments and offences that I had picked up along the way. I had gotten to this place through the neglect of something that I had been taught and had practiced faithfully early in my journey of following Jesus. In this moment of reflection, the words, ***"They made me a keeper of the vineyards, but my own vineyard I have neglected," Song of Solomon 1:6b BSB*** were certainly true of the state of my heart. Thankfully, in that very moment, God gave me grace. Grace to not harden my heart and blame others but rather to humble myself, soften my heart towards Him and walk back to the place that I had deserted, a place that He had chosen for me.

By the grace that God supernaturally poured on us in that season I began to seek His help in getting back to the place I had drifted from.

Looking back now, I can see that from that season onwards the Lord has led me back to a place of keeping my heart well-watered. Through this journey God helped me uproot the weeds of offence, insecurity, and busyness that had been growing unchecked in my heart for a while. This water also helped me become fruitful in bringing others to salvation and leading them to deal with their weeds. Having been on both sides of this state (a dry heart and a well-watered one) I can say that there is so much power and life in following Jesus with a well-watered heart. I never want to go back to the place of living and ministering from a dry heart because I learned that *'weeds easily overwhelm a person when their heart is dry.'* This is the experience and understanding with which I share this chapter with you. I've learnt that it is truly the water of the Spirit and the water of the Word that nourishes and nurtures the garden of our hearts. It is an essential ingredient to the fruitfulness of every person who has committed their life to following Jesus and that includes you.

The Power of Water

Water is the most essential element in a garden. We all know its importance for plant growth. However, the importance of water extends beyond just helping plants grow. Water is an essential ingredient for dealing with weeds. Of all the trouble that weeds give a farmer, there is one thing against which they are powerless. Weeds are powerless against water. Because of this, every time a farmer must deal with stubborn roots in his garden, one of the go-to tools available to him is water. A wise farmer uses water generously in his garden knowing that by keeping his garden well-watered two things happen.

- **The Water Nurtures and Nourishes the Plants-** It is an essential ingredient for their growth. It is so essential that in most instances the amount of water a plant receives is the difference between life and death as well as fruitfulness and a lack of it.
- **The Water Softens the Ground-** Heidi Strawn from hobbyfarms. com said it this way, *"Be sure to weed after rain or irrigation to ensure soft soil and aid in the removal of the entire weed. Leaving root pieces behind often ensures the weed's return."*

By helping you remove the entire weed's root, water enables the farmer to deal with weeds effectively!

In the natural, water can be seen as a double-edged sword in the battle to be fruitful. It is effective on weeds as well as on the crops. This picture helps us understand how it works spiritually. In the heart of a believer, this water that softens the ground, gives us a significant advantage over weeds and also promotes fruitfulness is the Holy Spirit and the Word of God (the Bible). And isn't it interesting that *Ephesians 6:17NLT teaches us that, "the (double edged) sword of the Spirit, ... is the word of God." {emphasis added by the author}.* The Holy Spirit and the Bible (the Word of God) working together are, to our hearts, what water is to natural gardens. Therefore, in order to effectively deal with weeds, we must diligently keep our hearts watered. We need to learn how to keep our hearts watered with the water of the Spirit and the water of the Word. Let's discuss each of these two expressions of water in the heart of a believer to understand them a little further.

The Water of The Word

Jesus said to his disciples in *John 15:3 TPT, "The words I have spoken over you have already cleansed you."* How was it possible for them to be purified by listening to words? Because these words were no ordinary words, they were (and still are) the water of the Word of God. They are tremendously powerful! Hebrews 4:12 tells us that these words, which are the Word of God, are quick, powerful, and sharp. That is why meditating on them is so good for us. Jesus' disciples had been listening to and meditating on all that He had been speaking to them. And though they didn't fully understand it all yet, it was already active in their hearts, purifying them of weeds simply because they had been willing to make room for it. They weren't like the others who had closed their hearts and deserted Him when He began sharing with them the more challenging truths of the Word of God. By making this room for the Word of God in their hearts, they allowed their hearts to be watered by the Divine Gardener. In the same way, by making room for the Word of God in your heart, you receive living water for the garden of your life.

Because the Word cleans, it reveals! This is what Hebrews 4:12 means when it continues to tell us that the Word of God, *"Exposes our innermost thoughts and desires." NLT.* Interestingly, this happens in a natural garden as well. When the garden is dry, weeds and plants somehow begin to look a bit similar. Because dryness makes everything a little lifeless, it becomes challenging to fully make out the differences sometimes. But the moment rain or irrigation washes their leaves and revives the life in them, there is no mistaking what a weed is. This is what the Word of God, as water, does to our hearts. It gives us life while simultaneously exposing to us things in our hearts that are weeds. This revelation is not given to shame us for struggling with weeds but to help us overcome them. So, when you read the Bible and feel exposed, always remember that you are also receiving grace through the Spirit. (We will look at the water of the Holy Spirit in depth in the next section)

Among Jesus' twelve disciples, there was, however, one who heard the words of Jesus but didn't allow them to penetrate his heart. What was the result? The weed of the love of money drove him to the sin of betraying Jesus and eventually to committing suicide. This shows us that the Word must not only be heard, but it must also be obeyed.

Developing The Practice of Reading the Bible

As we develop this practice of reading the Bible, what matters most is the place from which we're doing it in our hearts. Because of this, we need to manage the tension between our devotion to God and following rules and man-made religion. Rules and religion have received a bad reputation over the past couple of years in Christian circles, but they are not all bad. They are essential in helping us build consistency. We need this consistency for our Bible reading practice to benefit us. When we lack consistency, it hinders us from being rooted and grounded in the Word of God and many times is the first step towards our Bible reading plan dying a slow but certain death. So, yes, we need consistency in our practice of reading the Bible. However, that consistency can't come only from a place of rules and man-made religion otherwise it will be lifeless.

Devotion is what gives this practice life. It opens the door for our Bible reading to grow our relationship with God. Because of this, devotion to God must always remain central to why we read our Bibles (and pray) every day. The solution therefore is to start from devotion without completely ignoring the need for consistency. Consistency will come as a natural overflow of us maturing as we devote ourselves to God. In other words, we must aim for consistency without being enslaved to it. Through devotion we can ultimately grow and flow to a place where we gain the desired consistency and rhythm. In many ways, devotion can be seen as the source of the river, with consistency being the outflow of it. Looking back at my earlier practice of reading the Bible and praying, this may have been one of the things I needed to learn. I was a lot more rules and religion oriented, and I did not develop my practice out of a devotion to the Lord. My consistency may have focused more on rules and less on devotion and, because of that, when it was tested it failed me.

This tension between building devotion and managing consistency must be managed well- with a pure heart and clear conscience; with an emphasis on love and relationship that doesn't deny or dismiss the need for discipline and arduous work. It's just like it is between two people who love each other. They send and read each other's texts because they love and are devoted to each other. As that love grows, you can be sure that the frequency of the texting will increase (I hear my wife and I shouting hallelujah in the background). Of course, they need to be intentional in planning how and when they will do it. It would be foolish for them to completely ignore the need to schedule it. But the more important thing to realise is that in healthy relationships people text and read each other's text not because they have to, but because they choose to. Frequency and intentionality are the result of genuine love and affection, not fear induced rules and religion. Dawson Trotman expressed it this way, ***"Discipline imposed from the outside eventually defeats when it is not matched by desire from within."***

What does this mean for us believers? It means we should read the Bible not because we have to but because we choose to. You see, when we choose something with our freewill, we grow in love with it. The act of choosing it configures our mind to treasure and be devoted to it. And the more consistently we choose it, the deeper our devotion will be to that thing. As we build our desire from within, the discipline that we impose from the outside will not be defeated by the trials and storms of life. This is how true love grows and matures. Not that we have to, but that we choose to. Once the approach is from the right place, our Bible reading habit comes alive. And anything that is alive grows. So, it follows that when our Bible reading becomes life giving it will grow not just in consistency but in depth as well. It is this consistency and depth that will help bring us into a rich and life-giving relationship with Jesus. Done right, reading the Bible is one of the cornerstones of fruitfulness in the life of a believer. It results in organic growth that helps us keep our gardens watered by the Word of God and that creates a perfect environment for uprooting weeds.

The Water of the Spirit

He Softens Hearts; The Holy Spirit is the rain that God promised to pour upon the last day Church (the Church you and I are a part of). This promise, found in *Acts 2:17 NLT* declares that *"In the last days,' God says, 'I will pour out my Spirit upon all people."* As this promised Spirit is poured out, He has the same effect on your heart that rain has on dry ground. He softens it. This means once you have identified a weed that is active in your heart, through a revelation from God's Word, you must guard against trying to uproot it in your own strength. This would be the equivalent of a farmer zealously trying to uproot weeds while his garden is dry. The consequence of this action is that most of the roots will break and remain in the ground resulting in them growing again once the conditions become favourable.

Instead, the wise thing to do is invite the water of the Holy Spirit to rain on that area of your life. This means bringing it to the Lord in prayer. The Spirit does the work in your heart that water does in the soil. He will help you soften your heart, making it possible to remove even the roots that go down so deep into your heart you don't fully understand them. He is able not only to help you get there but also to help you get them out. The key to experiencing this is to allow yourself to be led by Him. This is what Paul means when he says, *"Let the Holy Spirit guide your lives. Then you won't be doing what your sinful nature craves." Galatians 5:16 NLT* As you follow His leading you can be assured that your effort will result in completely uprooting the weeds from your heart. The pathway won't always be what you expected but the fruit will always be good at the end of it all.

One of the names of the Holy Spirit is Counsellor. A counsellor helps you process pain, hurt and other life experiences until you get to the root of the issues you need to deal with. When this happens, psychologists call it a breakthrough. They call it a breakthrough because they know, through study and experience, that this is where the healing begins. In the very same way, the Holy Spirit is a counsellor given to us by Jesus to help us get to the root of our issues. He (unlike human counsellors) is never wrong. When you sense His promptings in your heart concerning an issue, God, by His mercy, is not only revealing the roots of your struggle, but He is also giving you the grace to uproot it. *'Every time God brings your attention to an issue in your life, He is also simultaneously making available grace that is needed to deal with it.'* Make sure you take it because that is how the water of the Word and the water of the Spirit work together to make us fruitful. This cycle has the effect of keeping our hearts soft and tender towards Jesus.

Living A Spirit-Led Life

As I encourage you to yield yourself to the leading of the Holy Spirit, here are three postures of the heart that I would like to invite you to adopt. These postures create an atmosphere that is conducive for the water of the Spirit to flow in your life, your home, your business (yes, the Spirit can move in our businesses too) and, of course, the church.

- Posture 1: Holy Spirit move **however** you choose
- Posture 2: Holy Spirit use **whomever** you choose
- Posture 3: Holy Spirit I'll go **wherever** you choose

You see, when asked, most of God's people will say, "I want the water of the Holy Spirit flowing in my heart." The same question though, when asked a little differently, often reveals a different posture in our heart attitudes. Through asking ourselves creatively about these three heart postures the true level of our thirst for the water of the Holy Spirit is revealed.

An example of this can be seen in a true story of missionaries who prayed to God for the water of the Holy Spirit to come to the location where they were serving. The Lord heard their prayers, granted their request, and indeed sent the rain of the Holy Spirit. However, the person that God chose to use to usher in this move of the Holy Spirit is someone that one of the missionary ladies in the prayer group felt was not qualified to be used by God. This caused her to become offended and, as a result, she rejected the very rain of the Holy Spirit that she had prayed for when it finally arrived. Obviously, this hindered her from experiencing this revival that she had in fact prayed for. This is an example of how we can say we want the Holy Spirit with our mouths and even seek it through prayer and yet still have a heart posture that is not ready to receive it. In this instance it is clear to see that one of those who prayed for the water of the Holy Spirit did not posture her heart with the attitude of humility that says, "Holy Spirit use whomever you choose!"

Therefore, we can see that the key is to pray not only that the Holy Spirit would come but that God would give us the grace to have a heart that is ready to receive Him when He shows up. A heart humble enough to receive Him through the vessel that He chooses to flow. Building these three heart postures is essential because they are the key to experiencing the rain of the Holy Spirit when the Lord chooses to send it. History has shown that the Holy Spirit uses the most unlikely of mediums even to the point of speaking to a prophet using a donkey. (Numbers 22:8) He is ready and willing to lead us. Our heart posture is the x-factor here. It is the key to experiencing breakthroughs in our lives. So, I would like to invite you to reject the spirit of apathy, lethargy and indifference that is plaguing our generation. Instead, I encourage you to be thankful for the gift of the Holy Spirit recognising that:

1. *"We are all privileged to drink deeply of the same Holy Spirit."* *1 Corinthians 12:13, TPT*
2. *"Those who drink the water I (Jesus) give will never be thirsty again. John 4:14a* **NLT (emphasis added by the author)** &
3. *"It (the water of the Spirit) becomes a fresh, bubbling spring within them (YOU), giving them (YOU) eternal life." John 4:14b* **NLT (emphasis added by the author)**

As you can see, both these practices (Reading the Word of God and communion with the Holy Spirit through prayer) are important in equal measure. One cannot replace the other. We need both of them at work in our lives in a balanced way as we make every effort to keep our hearts watered. Charles Spurgeon, an English Puritan Baptist preacher from the 19th century expressed it this way, ***"When asked, 'what is more important: praying or reading the Bible?' I ask, 'what is more important: breathing in or breathing out?'*** Done well, with the right balance and the right approach, reading the Bible and praying every day is the key to keeping our hearts well-watered in the journey of following Jesus. And a well-watered garden gives its farmer the best possible chance to successfully remove weeds and be fruitful.

Signs Of a Dry Heart

As we conclude, I would like to highlight some signs and symptoms that point us to a dryness of our hearts. These signs could be pointers to more than just a dry heart, but it is unlikely that they would be present in a person's life if their heart is well-watered. Each of these signs almost always fizzles and eventually dies away as we put into practice the habit of reading our Bibles daily and communing with the Holy Spirit in prayer. One of the words that the Bible uses to describe this dryness is lukewarm (Revelation 3:16) and I'll use the same word in most of my descriptions of these signs. Being lukewarm is being indifferent where God calls us to be passionate, committed, resolute and devoted. Here are examples of signs that point to this.

- Being indifferent where God calls us to be passionate. (For example, being lukewarm during praise and worship)
- Being absent where God requires us to be present. (For example, lukewarm about regular communal gatherings with other believers.)
- Being silent where God calls us to speak (for example lukewarm about telling others about Christ)

These are just a few examples of the lukewarmness that occurs in a dry heart. If you see any of these symptoms in yourself, take heart. Remember, you can overcome it. You can water your heart and revive the passion that you once had for God. A passion that doesn't just keep you in His service it helps you get better as you serve Him. A passion that also empowers you to successfully remove weeds from your life. Just like water is the most essential element in a natural garden, the Spirit and the Word are the most essential elements for living a fruitful life.

Reflection.

*When looking at the signs of a dry heart, are there any that are present In your life right now?

Yes ☐   No ☐

*Having read this chapter, what one step do you think you can take to begin or continue the journey of living your life with a well-watered heart?

_____

_____

_____

_____

_____

Chapter 12

✳

Conclusion

***To do something big, just commit to doing something
small every day until you achieve the big thing.***

Character is formed in the school of discipline.
(Dr Brian J Bailey)

Concluding Thoughts on The Journey of Dealing with Weeds

I would like to share two concluding thoughts as you continue on your
journey of dealing with weeds:

1. Commit yourself to a repeatable routine and
2. Love your garden.

These two keys provide ideas that I believe will help you put into
practice all that you have learned from this book.

Commit To a Repeatable Routine

The value of routines is rarely in how long we do them when we finally get
to doing them but rather how often we actually get to do them. The value
of all you've learnt in this book is found more in how often you will apply

it, than how long you do it when you do apply it. This is why I would like to suggest to you as we come to the end of our journey together that you commit to a repeatable routine.

A repeatable routine is a minor change that I can realistically commit to in the hope of improving my life in some way. In order for it to be repeatable it must be small, realistic, and measurable. Throughout this book, there are challenges that may have prompted you to make a big shift in your life based on the new understanding that you have gained. Instead of thinking, "What momentous change can I make so that I can see drastic improvement in that area of my life? I encourage you to think, "What minor change can I make based on what I've learnt that I can maintain over an extended period of time?"

A repeatable routine is the kind of change that has the likelihood to last long enough for you to see its fruits. This is why I recommend that you commit to this kind of change when dealing with weeds. The fruit of changes in this area are reaped over time. Without repeatable routines, dealing with weeds is an up and down journey that is inconsistent at best, and delivers disappointment at worst. I would like to encourage you to approach dealing with weeds from the mentality of setting up repeatable routines in your life instead of big spontaneous commitments that make a show but do not help you grow and maintain strength in the long run.

Let's use the thought of retracing your steps personally as an example. If you feel that this is something you need to put into practice, ask yourself, *"What one change can I make today that I can repeat tomorrow to help me retrace my steps?"* Keep in mind that no change is too small as long as it is a positive change. You may decide to start spending five minutes a day thinking through how your day went before going to bed. In those five minutes you can spend time reflecting and asking yourself if there are some offences that you need to let go of or if there are some unresolved issues that you need to revisit and resolve. Five minutes really does not seem like much, but let's do the math for a moment to see the impact of these five minutes on your life. If you faithfully maintain your commitment to this routine and repeat it daily, five minutes daily becomes 35minutes per week. 35minutes per week becomes 30.3 hrs a year. What is the lesson in this illustration? Start small so that you can repeat the routine long enough to benefit from it. Starting small also enables you to build the muscle needed to do that routine for a longer amount of time in the future if necessary. I recommend that you start small, repeat often, and allow growth in how long you do it to come naturally. The secret to most life change is in starting routines that we can repeat long enough to benefit from them. This is because, almost always in life, we benefit from routines over a period of time, not from a moment in time. The moments in time are sparks and catalysts to get us going but true change happens in the marathon. Lasting change is the result of repeated processes. So, whatever you've committed to do, I urge you to do it sustainably. You will benefit more from it that way.

Love Your Garden

Going into my garden and doing the actual weeding is arduous work. It's painful on my back, the sun is often beating me down as well. Oftentimes all my arduous work seems to be making little difference. It feels like there's a lot more work to be done even though I've already done so much work already. In light of this, I ask myself, *"What keeps the farmer going?" "What keeps him motivated in spite of the apparent lack of progress?" "" What keeps him working in spite of the physical and emotional exhaustion?"* The love for his garden is what keeps a farmer going.

If a farmer loses the love he has for his garden, the practice of weeding and tending to his garden will die a natural death. In the same way, if we find that we are more comfortable telling others about what to do in their gardens while neglecting our own garden we must search ourselves to see if we still love our garden. Do we still have a passion to be fruitful; to be all that God called and designed us to be? Is our love for God still fresh or has it grown cold? We must realise that, ultimately, our garden represents our relationship with Jesus. Therefore, fruitfulness in our garden is linked closely to our relationship with Jesus. This is spelt out clearly in John 15 where Jesus teaches us, ***"No branch can bear fruit by itself; it must remain in the vine. Neither can you bear fruit unless you remain in me." John 15: 4b NIV*** To be fruitful, we must stay in love with Jesus because separate from him we can produce nothing of eternal value. To be motivated to deal with our weeds, a love for our garden is essential. And that love is born from a love relationship with Jesus; from a daily choice to keep him at the centre of our lives. Dealing with weeds is simply about taking things out of our lives that Jesus doesn't want to be there- and those are the things that hamper our fruitfulness. Jesus is the one who knows what must not be there. He is the one who tells me what a weed is and what isn't. Therefore, I must constantly be listening to Him. He alone knows the secret to fruitfulness in my life and He will guide me into it. So, a genuine love for the person of Jesus Christ is absolutely at the centre of me dealing with weeds and living a fruitful life.

This means I do what he says not out of obligation, but out of a love for him. I love him not for what I can get out of Him, but because He loved me first and gave his life to rescue me. This also means I trust him to lead me into the fullness of what God created me to be. I love him not just because it is the right thing to do. I love him not out of a fear that if I don't, I'll end up in hell. No! I love Him because I choose to pour out my love and my life to the one who saved my soul, to the one who chose to lay down His life so I could live mine to the full.

That is why I love Jesus.
That is why I love my garden.
That is why I weed my garden.

Conclusion

This is just the beginning. It's not the end. These are the few observations that I made about the qualities of weeds in nature. These qualities teach us about weeds that can occur in the garden of our spiritual lives. I'm sure that there are many more qualities of weeds that we can learn from, and I encourage you to continue to do so. The ones I have chosen to share in this book are the ones that were shown to me in my journey of learning to deal with weeds. As you can see, with each quality comes a new insight of how we can deal with weeds in our own hearts. I hope I've inspired you to continue to learn from nature how spiritual weeds can affect the garden of your life as well as ways in which you can weed them out.

May your journey in dealing with weeds, whether in the natural garden or the spiritual garden of your heart cultivate and perfect in you Jesus Christ. May you remain in Him all the days of your life and experience the

Lungile Ncube

fullness of His promise that, *"Those who remain in me, and I in them, will produce much fruit." John 15:5b NIV*

The Lord Bless You and Keep You in The Garden of His Love, Amen!

The end!

Printed in the United States
by Baker & Taylor Publisher Services

Printed in the United States
by Baker & Taylor Publisher Services